Editorial

Warriors, craftswomen and... Vikings

Investigating the surge in women-focused coworking spaces is an unprecedented initiative in Europe. This immersion in the heart of the continent's most hitherto unknown working communities is even ethnographic in nature. For 6 months, I have met the founders, facilitators and members of 22 coworking spaces established in 14 cities across 10 countries.

I ventured into the flip side of the flattering mirror of *Instagram* to experience these very different places and to scrutinize every detail, bearing in mind the sketch of my own coworking project in the Paris region. I took a seat in the open spaces to work alongside my colleagues and question them. I was struck by their entrepreneurial energy and their determination to break down stereotypes.

Every day, these women invent ways of working, learning and collaborating that give shape to sisterhood in dedicated work environments, the rules of which they determine themselves. However, the creation of these safe spaces and the management of their communities is not done without trial and error, and is also a constant struggle for acceptability, profitability and sustainability.

Whether they call themselves *Patronnes*, #girlboss, chicks, badass or even *Vikings*, they claim their unique identity with strength, pride and a certain casualness. In a context still marked by sexism, they hope to conquer a fairer place in society by gathering and sticking together. Whether in heels or sneakers, they are striving – each in their own way – for a more open and inclusive future of work. For these women warriors and artisans – whether they are entrepreneurs, freelancers, self-employed or in professional transition – women-focused coworking spaces offer an unprecedented training and base camp.

Will you dare to join the movement?

Ivanne Poussier
CEO & Co-Founder
Ada Coworking

Summary

Primer about the overall context and the methodology behind our investigation

Strategic section to apprehend the phenomenon from a global point of view

User-centric approach useful for designing a project and drawing on best practices

Gold mine for project owners and managers of coworking spaces in activity

Facts & Ideas
gleaned throughout the pages

The sudden rise of women-focused coworking spaces coincided with the #MeToo
movement of 2017 which massively denounced sexual and sexist violence against women.
p.10

We estimate that there are about 50 women-focused coworking spaces across
the continent, wether they are shared offices or workshops, coworking spaces with babycare
or childcare, feminist coworking spaces, women only social clubs. p.13

The epicenter of this phenomenon is located between London, Berlin, Zurich and Paris. p.18

The smallest women-focused coworking space in Europe is French and is just 30sqm. p.23

When members are asked what color they would like to see
on the wall, pink is far from a consensual choice. p.24

The variety of concepts makes it possible to identify at least 6 different models. p.26

It was in Milan that a pioneering academic team addressed for the first time the issue
of gender in the workplace with an interdisciplinary approach. p.32

Rehabilitating women on their return to the labor market after maternity leave:
this is the mission of the sisters Panni and Kata Klementz in Budapest. p.37

In 30% of the spaces of our sample, the CEO or at least one member
of the management team is of foreign nationality. p.39

Women are on average less satisfied than men with both their usual workplace
and alternative third places. The proportion of women is 40% among coworkers
and 38% among leaders of coworking spaces (owners or founders). p.40

The main reproaches formulated against male coworkers point to rather trivial habits
and incivilities. p.43

In our view, the quest for a sustainable women-focused coworking model will
be played out on two main fronts. First, the community front, which will be about creating,
developing and maintaining customer loyalty over the long term. Second, the financial front,
which is based on an effective diversification of activities and ultra rigorous management. p.59

A coworking community can also thrive without walls, as in Dublin, by organizing itinerant
meetings at (mixed) partner coworking spaces, alternating with virtual events. p.66

Introduction
From the Atlantic to the Baltic

Created by women, for women and their allies, women-focused coworking spaces are flourishing all over Europe. Some are exclusively female – much like some gym chains – and others are open to all. Under a variety of brands and concepts, they address the issue of gender in workplaces of the future – a landscape increasingly marked by the rise of entrepreneurship, freelancing and new ways of working.

This global phenomenon has become increasingly popular in Europe since 2017 following the dazzling irruption of the US market leaders, The Wing (2016) and The Riveter (2017).

In 2019, I partnered with Eva Bordachar, a digital entrepreneur like me, to open our women-focused coworking space in the suburbs of Paris, north of the Yvelines. After having experienced the limits of the more traditional coworking offers available to us, we identified with interest this niche segment, which was already particularly well-publicized in the US. What a surprise: a quick online search revealed the existence of at least thirty of these spaces in no less than 12 European countries! Faced simultaneously with the drafting of our business plan and this abundance of women-focused coworking spaces, I undertook the European Tour of Women's Coworking Spaces for 6 months.

But the purpose of this field survey is not limited to studying the market by comparing different business models and identifying best practices. Our ambition in publishing this book is to open the discussion on the new collaborative places and ways of working that are necessary for the development of today's and tomorrow's digital female talents, as well as to highlight initiatives designed to meet the specific needs of female entrepreneurs and freelancers.

This introduction reviews the context in which the European Tour of Women's Coworking Spaces took place, before detailing the investigation method used and the sample of coworking spaces studied.

Photo by Michał Parzuchowski on Unsplash

A niche market pioneered by the United States

The global phenomenon of coworking, which appeared at the turn of the 2000s, is now reaching maturity in urban centers after a decade-long ramp-up from 2005 to 2015.

In Europe, the market is expected to continue to grow. The most mature metropolitan areas are seeing the emergence of new coworking concepts geared to a specific sector or profile (photographers, musicians, designers, digital nomads, etc.).

Among the new user segments targeted by coworking spaces are women or young mothers (and young fathers). Relatively under the radar until 2016, this niche segment has experienced spectacular growth since 2017.

Two pioneers: *The Wing* and *The Riveter*
The nebula of women-focused coworking spaces was pioneered by two American leaders with a very large audience both in the media and on social networks.

The Wing, co-founded in 2016 in New York City by Audrey Gelman, former press secretary to Hillary Clinton, raised $117.5 million. To date, there are 11 spaces already open and 5 more are announced for 2020. According to *INC.* the brand had nearly 500,000 online followers in 2019, extending its influence far beyond its cities of operation.

The Riveter, co-founded in 2017 in Seattle by attorney Amy Nelson, raised $21.6 million and has nine spaces to date.

Spaces powered by women all around the world
Other brands soon appeared simultaneously all over the world: in Canada, Mexico, Brazil, Australia, New Zealand, Japan, etc.

The debate is far from settled between female-only – reserved for an exclusively female clientele – and female-focused – conceived by women and open to all. We will try to establish a more precise typology in the following section (*Overview*).

But what they all have in common is that they are founded and run by women, who are still too under-represented in the coworking sector. On average, the proportion of women is 40% among coworkers and 38% among coworking leaders, whether they are owners or founders (*Deskmag*, 2019).

To federate these professionals, in 2016 two Americans, Laura Shook-Guzman and Iris Kavanagh, created an international association of women coworking space founders and co-founders, *Women Who Cowork (WWCO)*. Their tagline: "*The future of coworking is female*".

A sudden blossoming of European coworking concepts
The European market has undergone a major shift since 2017, with the emergence of some thirty female coworking projects in three years, i.e. about ten new locations per year, compared with an average of two per year at the beginning of the decade 2010 (see graph).

At this brisk pace, the landscape is being enriched with a wide variety of coworking concepts, for example, single coworking brands taking root in several addresses. In Germany, for instance, the first *CoWomen* coworking space opened in Berlin in 2018 and then a second one followed in Heidelberg in 2019.

In the Netherlands, Emilie Sobels created two coworking spaces in Amsterdam in 2015 under the *#Workmode* brand, before extending her network to Utrecht, Rotterdam and Groningen, with one new address per year.

In parallel with this movement of grassroots emergence was the arrival of American brands such as the **Hera Hub** franchise in Uppsala, Sweden (August 2017) and **The Wing** in London (October 2019). For some time, *The Wing* had intentions of expanding to a private mansion in the trendy neighborhood of *Le Marais* in Paris, but despite much publicity, the plans never came to fruition.

Meanwhile, in 2019 the female-only business club **Allbright** expanded from London (where it already has two spaces) across the Atlantic to the United States after raising $18.8 million. With its Hollywood location, it is the only example to date of a European coworking concept being exported outside the continent. ●

Chronology of an accelerated outbreak since 2017

Number of openings per year

& openings planned for the first half of 2020

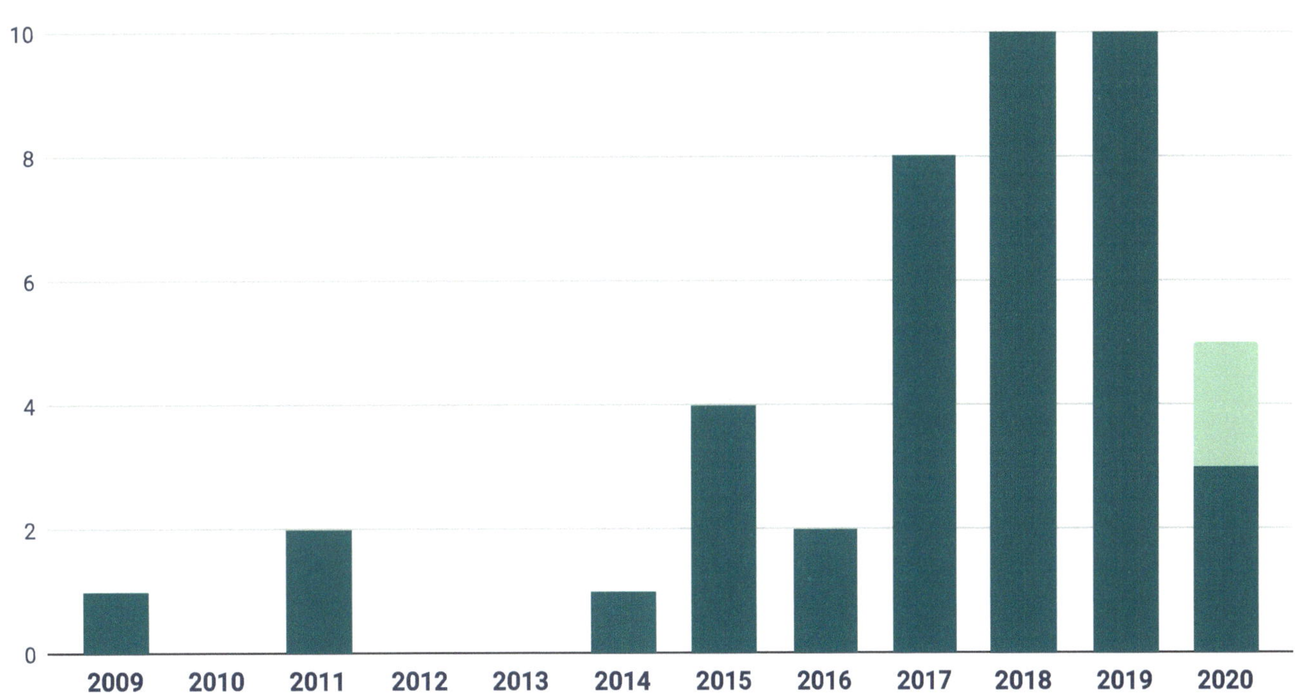

Openings of women-focused coworking spaces and identified projects as of March 1, 2020 verified by direct contact (total: 43). The rhythm of 10 annual openings could stall in 2020 because of the Covid-19 epidemic, before starting again in 2021.

Photo by CoWomen (Berlin) on Unsplash.

A movement destined to mark the decade 2020

The sudden rise of women-focused coworking spaces coincided with the **#MeToo** movement of 2017 which massively denounced sexual and sexist violence against women.

More than just workplaces, these working communities offer an alternative to a sexist work culture that is still slow to evolve. The new economy is no more spared than the old one, as proven by an investigation conducted by American journalist Emily Chang in Silicon Valley. In 2017 she revealed the gloomy underside of the *"bro culture"* that reigns there in a hard-hitting book entitled **Brotopia: Breaking Up the Boys' Club of Silicon Valley.**

By focusing on women's empowerment, women-focused coworking spaces – although controversial for recreating the closed clubs they themselves denounce – nevertheless provide concrete answers to major concerns:

- Women's participation in the labour market (orientation, employability);

- Female entrepreneurship (education, networking, access to financing and investment);

- Better time conciliation between professional and personal life (balance, taking into account parenthood);

- Promotion of female role models and fight against discrimination.

Women-focused coworking spaces assert themselves as the crucibles of a future of work paradoxically more open and inclusive. Their vocation is to become permanently established in the landscape. ●

Six months of field survey

Having carried out an online census of some 30 coworkings spaces, we started a 6-month tour of Europe. Our objective was not only to experience them concretely but also to immerse ourselves in their communities by meeting those who make them, animate them and use them.

We visited 22 spaces and conducted interviews in each of them. We supplemented these immersive experiences with remote interviews with the leaders of 8 other spaces, bringing our sample to a total of 30 spaces. We also met with 3 researchers and 7 experts to enrich our analysis with multidisciplinary insights.

At the same time, we continued our census and completed the collection of data in order to shed light on this emerging phenomenon, resulting in a European online directory of women-focused coworking spaces, accessible on our website.

A plural subject of study

To begin with, what do we intend to study under the term "women-focused coworking spaces"? We refuse to equate this phenomenon with a purely aesthetic trend, claiming a certain boudoir-like conception of "femininity" based on the color pink, velvet or flowers, for example. This reductive image is unfortunately conveyed by numerous articles in the feminine press and lifestyle blogs devoted to the design and decoration of these places.

On closer inspection, the founders and owners claim a commitment to women's empowerment and inclusion more broadly, expressed in a wide variety of concepts and business models. In order to conduct a comparative analysis, we included both mixed and non-mixed spaces in our sample, all founded by women and with at least 40% female members (ideally between 50% and 100%).

The first online searches following these objective criteria revealed rich and stimulating offers:

- **shared office or workshop** for creatives and digital professionals;
- **coworking spaces with babycare** intended for young parents and used mostly by mothers;

Willa, incubator (Paris)

- **feminist coworking space** dedicated to women, lesbians, trans and non-binary people only, with activist projects;
- vegan **social club** or women-only **clubhouse** with restaurant, fitness room, spa and indispensable nail bar.

In our sample, coworking is generally the main vocation of the space, but we have also included examples where it is a secondary activity. These include *Willa*, an incubator in Paris and *cowBonne*, which forms part of a cultural space in Barcelona called *La Bonne*.

An ethnographic approach

What motivates women to create or join women-focused coworking spaces? How do they offer a differentiating experience compared to other coworking spaces? What impact do they have on female entrepreneurship and freelancing? How do they contribute to the empowerment of women in the future of work? Finally, can we characterize a European model?

Beyond the observation of physical workplaces (layout, equipment, decoration) and the comparative study of business models, this survey aims at identifying the user experience from two complementary angles:

- the individual experiences and trajectories of the members as well as of the leaders and their teams, who are the first users of these spaces;
- the collective dynamics at work: sense of community, learning and collaboration dynamics.

We opted for an immersion in these communities in order to experience them ourselves and then conduct interviews with the users.

We gave priority to cities with at least 2 spaces of interest such as Berlin, Zurich, London or Paris, then to geographical areas with a certain density of locations such as the Benelux countries, the Baltic Sea region and Spain.

To complete this field survey, the study sample was then enriched with remote interviews and abundant documentation, following the 3 steps detailed in the opposite sidebar.

Step 1. Immersions & visits

At the rate of 1 week per month over a period of 6 months, the immersions and visits represent a total of 30 days on the field. Here is the methodology used for each space:

- Initiating contact 3 to 4 weeks in advance to purchase a day pass and check the availability of the interlocutors;
- An average of 1 day of observation at a workstation, taking part in the life of the group at each occasion (coffee break, shared lunch, event);
- Otherwise, visit with interview for coworking areas that do not offer access for the day;
- Look & feel analysis of the user experience and additional research on the web (website, social networks, press…).

Step 2. Interviews & data collection

- Semi-directive on-site interviews with at least one manager or, if not available, one team member (22 spaces);
- Remote interviews to complete the sample with other existing, planned or closed coworking concepts (8 spaces);
- Creation of a quantitative and qualitative database (more than 45 spaces).

Step 3. Analysis

Our analysis is based on data from research papers in the humanities and social sciences, identified with the help of sociologist Olivia Chambard, a post-doctoral researcher at the *Centre d'études de l'emploi et du travail* (*Conservatoire National des Arts et Métiers*, Paris). We also interviewed 2 researchers and 7 experts in order to benefit from their insights and to deepen our analysis grid.

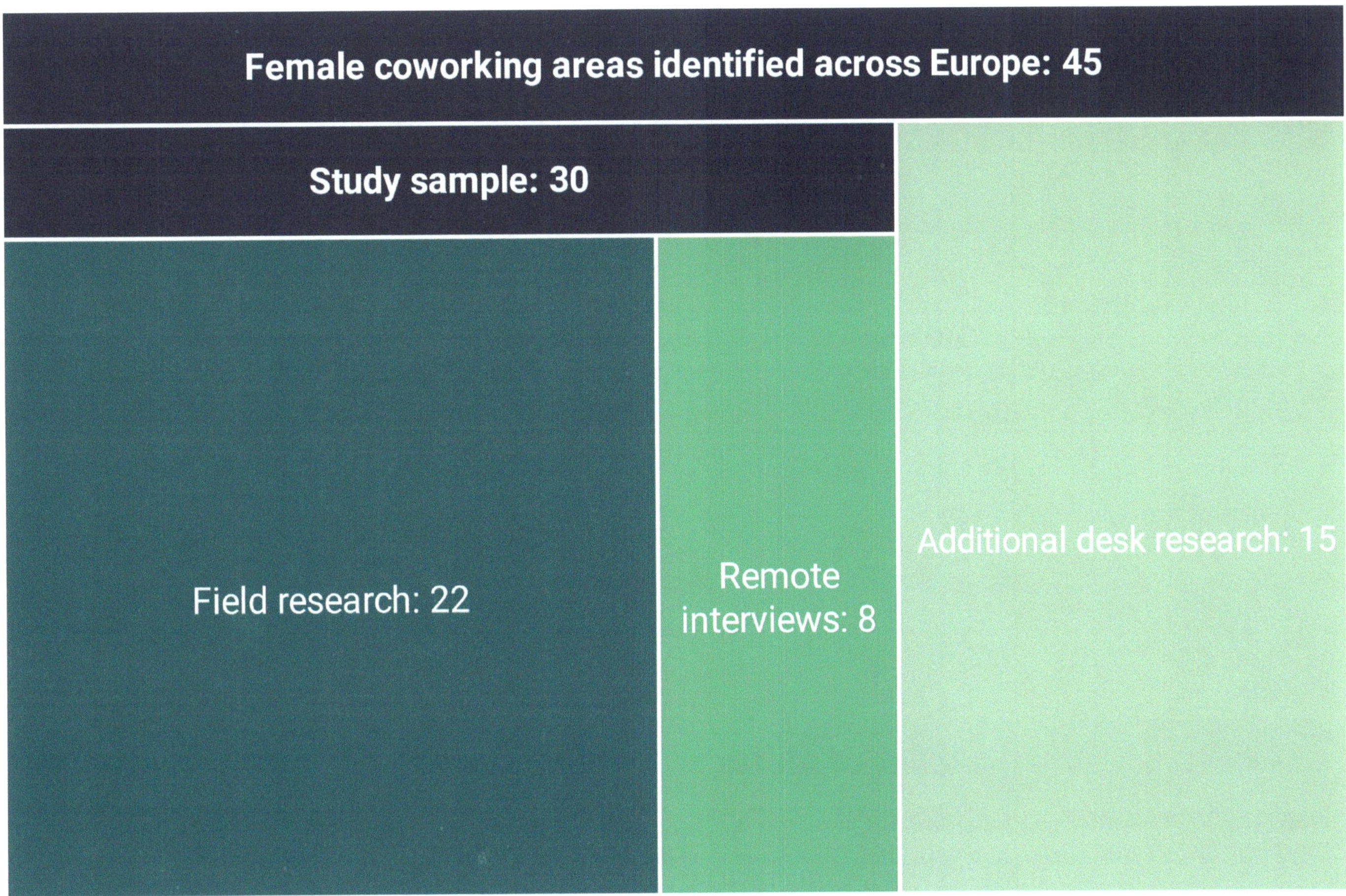

A representative sample of the European landscape

Our **database** includes a total of 45 women-focused coworking spaces identified and verified in 31 cities across 15 countries. We used them to identify major market trends. Unless otherwise stated, data is as of March 1, 2020.

This database is intended to be updated and progressively enriched by verifying the information available online through direct contact, bearing in mind that some informal or non-profit concepts such as shared offices or women's work collectives do not have a website of their own and do not actively publicize their existence.

Our **study sample** includes 30 spaces in 22 cities across 13 countries, covering 71% of the cities and 87% of the countries represented in our database. The majority of the sample is made up of spaces in operation (26 out of 30 or 87%). In order to understand different business models and analyze the entire life cycle of women-focused coworking spaces, we also studied:

- 1 space still in its initial phase of development in Brussels (**WOMADE**) whose founder we met during our immersion at *Girlsmode* in Antwerp;

- 1 experimental space that had just closed in Copenhagen (**W.e.Space**) and whose co-founder agreed to share with us "first hand" experience feedback;

- 2 temporary spaces, whose founders we interviewed a posteriori: ***Mona by My Little Paris*** in Paris (visited in 2017, before the survey) and ***Das Packhaus Heumarkt*** in Vienna. (the coworking space is still in activity but its experimental space dedicated to women has not been extended).

Contacted in anticipation of our leg in London, the clubs ***The Wing*** and ***Allbright*** did not follow up. However, we hope to have the opportunity to include them in a future edition.●

30 spaces
distributed in
22 cities
across
13 countries

CoWomen
Berlin (*Germany*)

JuggleHub
Berlin (*Germany*)

Wonder
Berlin (*Germany*) 

Hashtag Workmode
Rotterdam (*The Netherlands*)

Girlsmode
Anvers (*Belgium*)

Birdhaus
Zurich (*Switzerland*)

WeSpace
Zurich (*Switzerland*)

W.e. Space
Copenhagen (*Denmark*)

Blooming Founders
London (*United Kingdom*)

Cuckooznest
London (*United Kingdom*)

The Tribe
Totnes (*United Kingdom*)

Bonnie & Smile 
Paris (*France*)

La Patronnerie 
Paris (*France*)

L'Atelier Viking
Nantes (*France*)

Womade 
Brussels (*Belgium*)

Cowomen Heidelberg
Heidelberg *(Germany)*

[F]empower Stuttgart
Stuttgart *(Germany)*

SALON F
Munich *(Germany)*

Doors Open Female Hub
The Hague *(The Netherlands)*

Tadah
Zurich *(Switzerland)*

O4 Flow
Gdánsk *(Poland)*

Brain Embassy
Warsaw *(Poland)*

Hera Hub
Uppsala *(Sweden)*

Comunidad Nosotras
Madrid *(Spain)*

cowBonne
Barcelona *(Spain)*

Willa
Paris *(France)*

Mona by My Little Paris
Paris *(France)*

Das Packhaus Heumarkt
Vienna *(Austria)*

Loffice
Budapest *(Hungary)*

Women Co
Dublin *(Ireland)*

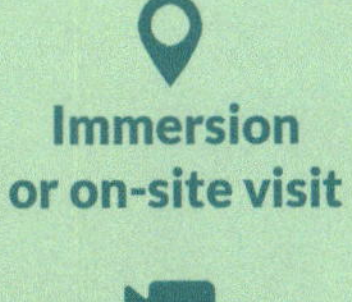

**Immersion
or on-site visit**

**Remote
interview**

Overview
Velvet revolution

In the shadow of the coworking giant *WeWork* and often influenced by the equally publicized precedent of *The Wing* from across the Atlantic, post-*Metoo* Europe has seen a quiet emergence of independent female coworking spaces. Few have heard of such spaces outside of their national borders, their only reference being the emerging female coworking concepts appearing in their own capital cities.

A better understanding of this up and coming niche market is found when we view it as a whole. First of all, cartography shows that it is widely distributed across the continent. While largely found in metropolitan areas, there has also been a notable breakthrough in medium-sized cities.

The analysis of names and logos then reveals brands full of boldness, both creative and committed, which play on codes and representations associated with femininity. Each of these brands attempts to encapsulate an original concept, articulating in a distinctive way a space, a bundle of services, events, and a community, and often involving a whole ecosystem of partners.

In order to grasp this multifaceted reality and make relevant comparisons, we propose a typology of women-focused coworking spaces in 6 main categories in order to explain the significant disparities in the key indicators analyzed.

This overview section sketches a first global vision of women-focused coworking spaces on a European scale, by characterizing no less than 6 reference models.

Mona (Paris) ®My Little Paris

An urban nebula across Europe

A snapshot as of March 1, 2020 reveals a market driven by **4 globalized cities**, London, Berlin, Zurich and Paris, **each comprising 2 or more spaces**. Brussels is expected to join them in 2020 with its first location having just opened in February, and plans for a second one currently underway.

Next come **15 political and economic capitals**: Amsterdam, Rotterdam, The Hague, Antwerp, Dublin, Oslo, Copenhagen, Warsaw, Gdánsk, Budapest, Vienna, Munich, Milan, Madrid and Barcelona. Hamburg should also join them in 2020.

Then, **9 dynamic regional capitals and medium-sized cities** stand out: Glasgow, Bristol, Nantes, Marseille, Utrecht and Groningen (Netherlands), Uppsala (Sweden), Stuttgart and Heidelberg (Germany).

Finally, it is worth noting the special case of **Totnes**, where *The Tribe* opened in January 2020 (40sqm, 8 seats). With fewer than 10,000 inhabitants, this transition town in southwest England aims at becoming self-sufficient in terms of energy and food. It is home to a number of self-employed women. Located six hours from London by train, it is the only rural coworking space in our sample. ●

Implantations of women-focused coworking spaces, clubs and communities identified, verified and contacted, including 2 temporary (in Paris and Vienna) and 2 recently closed (in Copenhagen and Glasgow), excluding projects, as of March 1, 2020 (total: 43).

Map created with Khartis, basemap from GISCO - Eurostat (European Commission).

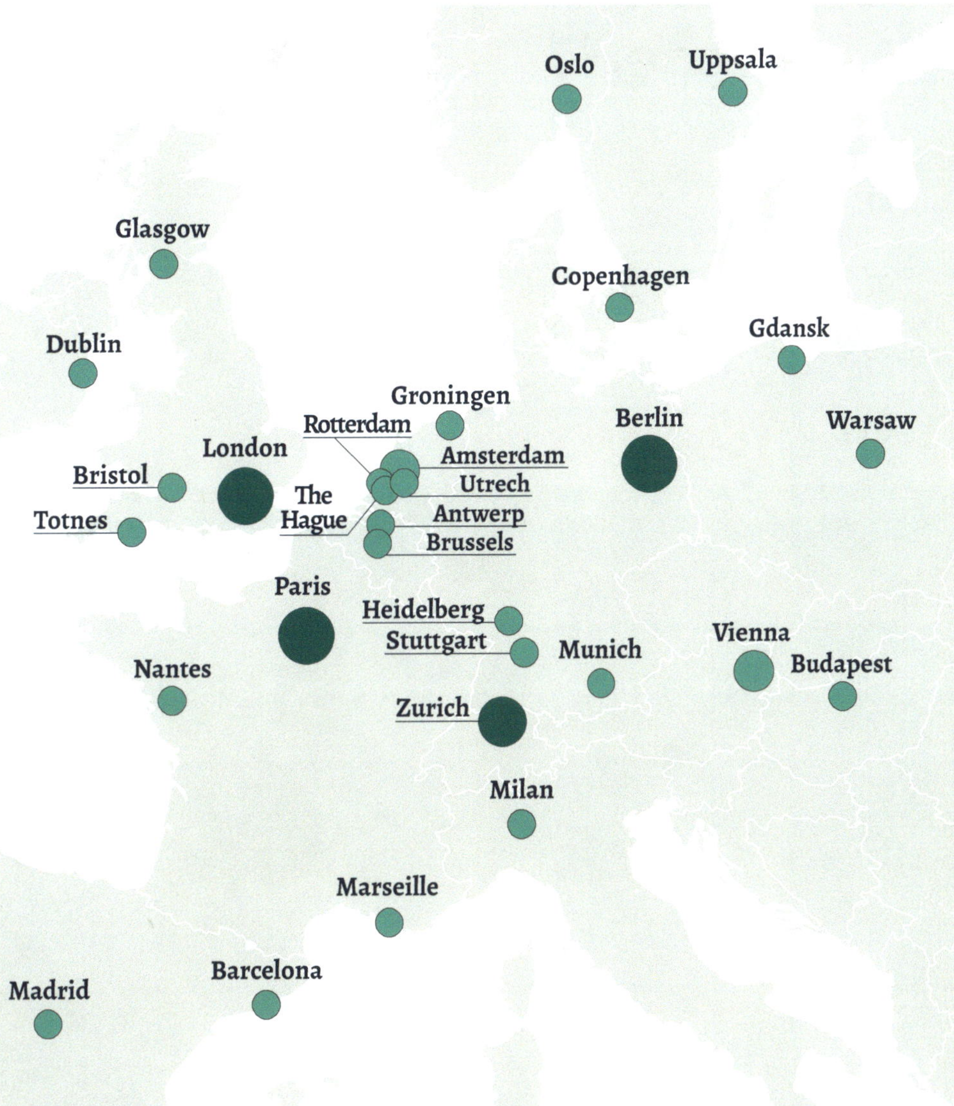

A phenomenon mainly concentrated in metropolitan areas

{Asserted brands}

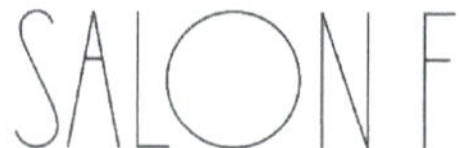

{Ambitious brands}

{Creative brands}

{Welcoming brands}

Brands full of audacity

Through their names, women-focused coworking spaces offer a plurality of approaches. Their logos offer a striking contrast. In an attempt to make sense of them, we have grouped the logos of 32 female coworking spaces on an illustration board (opposite) by classifying them according to 2 criteria: color (black or colored) and composition (name alone or together with a symbol).

Either rallying cries or coats of arms, these logos draw on multiple sources of inspiration to evoke the aspirations shared by the creators: community, mutual aid, sharing, learning, productivity, ambition, success, creativity, inclusion, and a balance between professional and personal lives.

Dedicated spaces

Women are evoked through the names *"girls"* and *"women"*, feminine pronouns (*nosotras*), acronyms (*W.e.* for *Women Entrepreneurs*, *F* for *Frauen*) and the first name *Mona* (see sidebar). In Paris, two daring neologisms stand out: *Willa*, the incubator that *"conjugates the will with the feminine"* playing on the English word *will/Will* (noun and masculine diminutive) and *La Patronnerie*, forged on the word *patronne* (meaning something like: *"bosses factory"*).

But what is perhaps more astonishing is the way in which the brands articulate the notion of space, emphasizing sometimes the shared work environment (*Atelier Viking, Loffice*), sometimes protection and intimacy (*Cuckooznest, Birdhaus*), and other times openness and connections (*Hera Hub, JuggleHub, Doors Open Female Hub*). Finally, combining this double dimension of intimacy and influence, *SALON F* in Munich refers to the tradition of women's clubs at the beginning of the 20th century in the United States.

Rallying cries

First, we've identified 8 brands with a black logotype that we call *"the assertive ones"*, such as the thundering *Tadah*. The choice of fonts is a reflection of these brands' bold attitudes (use of upper or lower case letters, bold fonts or

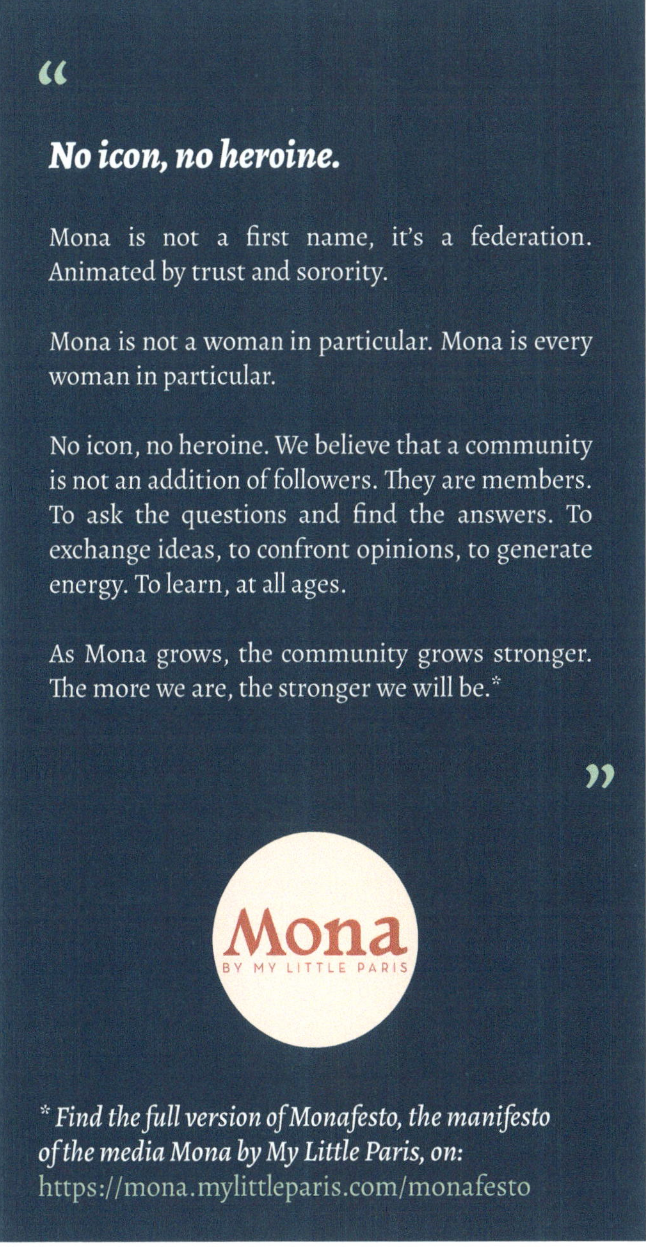

Girls just wanna have... flow!

"Flow" refers not only to the psychological definition (a state of mind when you focus on a pleasant activity) but also to a popular phrase in Polish. *"I've got the flow"* describes a kind of energy when you can feel the power and the ability to achieve something.

"Flow" applies perfectly to any woman entrepreneur who feels confident that she can do it even if she needs to close a gap and acquire new skills.

In addition, the flow also evokes the movement of the waves on the sea, right here on the coast of Northern Poland. In the same way with *O4 Flow*, our intent is to rise you up, far and beyond the seas, internationally!

Dominika Rossa
Head of O4 Flow (Gdánsk)

dynamic handwriting, very thick or, on the other hand, very thin characters).

Then there are 8 brands with a colorful logotype that we call *"ambitious brands"*. The most popular palette (after black & white) is made up of different blues, greens and blue-greens like the duck blue of **CoWomen** in Berlin or the blue-green gradient of **O4 Flow** in Gdánsk (see sidebar). These invigorating, optimistic colors are deliberately distanced from pink.

Feminine plural

Logos including logomarks, or symbols, on the other hand, largely use the rounded shape to evoke the community, inclusion and conviviality. Among them are 4 brands with an elaborate visual language. They can be read as coats of arms drawing plural representations of femininity and feminine ambition, far from the clichés traditionally associated with women (opposite).

We will later return in more detail to the visions of the founders and owners of these spaces, regarding the specific benefits associated with coworking among women. ●

Coats of arms

Atelier Viking in France refers to a barbarian people who shaped the identity of its territory, the city of Nantes on the Atlantic coast. The team of four leaders, who work on a voluntary basis, deploys a fierce spirit of conquest in the animation of this pocket-sized third place (30sqm), atypical in the local coworking ecosystem. Its co-founder, Pauline, expressed a desire to stand out from the clichés associating women with pink and meetings with *"girls' sleepovers"*. Sharing this casual approach, the first members quickly adopted the name *Viking*, when they don't call themselves *#meufs* or *#badass* on social networks.

WOMADE in Belgium (whose opening, scheduled for 2020, was confirmed to us at the time of writing) seizes the mythological figure of the mermaid. Its founder, Alba Pregja, explains that beyond her assumed beauty and seduction, the mermaid – the one in the tale – is one who follows her dreams. *"She is the perfect allegory of women's freedom and fierce independence. I also deliberately chose the color pink, to reclaim it and assert my feminist awareness."*

Hera Hub in Sweden summoned a deity from Ancient Greece, the goddess Hera – wife of Zeus and protector of women, their families and their financial security at every stage of their lives. Felena Hanson, the creator of the *Hera Hub* license in the United States wanted to *"find a name that had meaning but wasn't overtly feminine"*. The logo uses the *Hera* emblem, the peacock's feather, as a symbol of its beauty and prosperity. The feather appears stylized, either as an icon or to form the bar of the letter H on the logo.

The Tribe in the United Kingdom uses lunar symbolism that takes on its full meaning in the light of ancestral sacred traditions. Its founder, Stacey Sheppard, explains the choice of the tribe to evoke strength and power. She explains that she represented the three phases of the moon *"in that particular configuration as it represents the Triple Goddess and has been adopted by most Pagans, Wiccans, and Neopagans as a sacred symbol. It is said to represent the three phases of a woman's life: Maiden, Mother, Crone. For me, this was pretty well aligned to my ideal client. That's to say all women, of all ages, at all stages in their lives and businesses."*

Birdhaus (Zurich).

Is Millenial Pink really the new black?

We can find pink in only a handful of logos, whether it be nude pink (**Wonder**) or cotton candy pink (**WOMADE, Female Hub**). However, pink is indeed a part of the DNA of many women-focused coworking spaces, in both their graphic design and decoration.

Well-known to trend agencies, **Millennial Pink** is the pale salmon pink that appeared in Wes Anderson's film *The Grand Budapest Hotel* in 2014, and was later consecrated in 2015 with the nomination of **Quartz Pink** as color of the year by *Pantone*.

This color has been all the rage for half a decade with millennials – the generation born after 1980 – and on *Instagram*, many coworking spaces' preferred channel of communication. And it works. *"Don't underestimate the power of pink"* says

Ana Paula Tediosi, owner of **Birdhaus** in Zurich (photo). So has Millennial Pink really become the *"new black?'*

Controversial, revisited and re-appropriated pink

Pink is often presented in pale tones, warmed by golden touches and especially associated with contrasting colors (blue, white, black, anthracite). It's all about dosage. At **#Workmode** in Rotterdam, the longest wall wears a radiant golden yellow (photo). When the founder Emilie Sobels moved from the old premises, she asked the residents what they wanted to change or improve. The answer was unanimous: less pink! Three of the women with whom we spoke admitted to tolerating its presence as long as it was limited to small touches. The yellow colour was agreed upon unanimously.

For the co-founders of **WeSpace** in Zurich (photo), the initial choice of mint green – which is reflected in the decoration and the website – conveys a radical message aimed at deconstructing the stereotype that associates pink with femininity because it overlooks the diversity of talents, skills and ambitions among women.

About the use of pink in **CoWomen**'s graphic design as well as on the walls of the common room in their Berlin premises (photo), Hannah Dahl explains: *"It's not pink, it's peach!"* But at **CoWomen Heidelberg**, her colleague, Johannah Illgner, underlines the pink decorative touches when she shows us her small coworking space remotely and says to the webcam, half serious, half amused: *"Let's reclaim pink, after all!"* Ironic? Not so much.

Gender fluid

The matching of colors is as much a matter of taste as it is a matter of meaning. Driven by romanticism, western society has only associated pink with femininity since the 18th century, later resulting in little boys being dressed in blue and little girls in pink from the 19th century onwards. Previously, it used to be a powerful color, associated with men. The aristocrats went to war dressed in red and to the court dressed in pink, which was only a dim red: virile but stripped of its warlike character.

In the end, it doesn't matter whether these women choose pink, red, yellow, green or blue. Whether for its warlike character, or on the contrary its romantic character, or even in its new millennial hue known for its gender fluid nature, pink is just waiting to be interpreted, displayed in subtle shades and mixed in new palettes. Each of the founders we met seizes the language of colors to revisit it in her own way and invent her own code.

Hashtag Workmode (Rotterdam) by I. Poussier

WeSpace (Zurich)

CoWomen (Berlin) by Ana Torres

CoWomen Heidelberg by Sabine Arndt

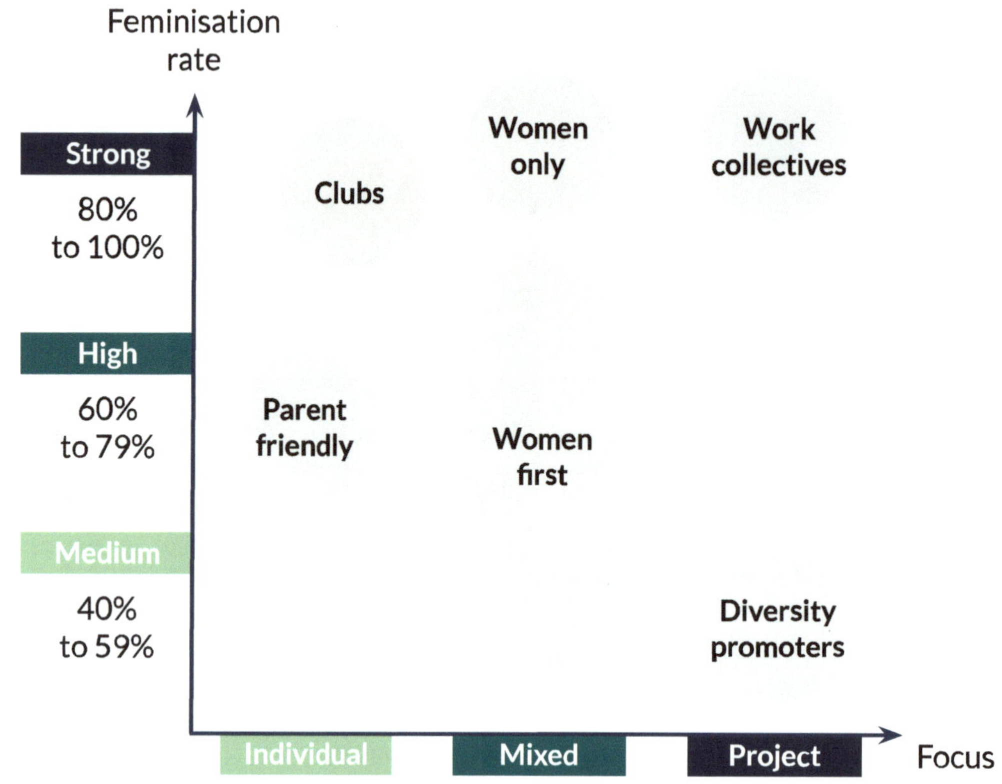

Six women-focused coworking models

Conjugating coworking with the feminine

Our typology of the different concepts of women-focused coworking spaces is based on two combined criteria, schematized on two axes (opposite).

Vertical axis: the feminization rate

Medium
The space reaches or exceeds gender parity if the share of women among the members is above 40% – the world average reported in the coworking industry according to *Deskmag* – and below 60% (the inversion point where men are in the minority).

High
Between 60% and 79%, women are visibly predominant on a daily basis.

Strong
From 80% female members, these spaces conditionally accept or tolerate the presence of men (which is rare or exceptional) and the rate reaches 100% if these spaces exclude men from their rules of procedure or membership process.

Horizontal axis: the focus

Focus on the individual:
These coworking spaces are primarily aimed at women with an emphasis on comfort, through equipment and services designed to ensure their physical and psychological well-being. They are positioned as an extension of the private sphere or as an in-between, facilitating the transition, articulation and balance between personal and professional life on a daily basis, notably by relieving them of what are presented as stressful tasks and concerns.

Focus on the project (entrepreneurship, art or activism):
These coworking spaces are aimed at entrepreneurs, freelancers, artists or activists, in the process of creating or developing a project. They give them visibility and are aimed at stimulating their economic and financial empowerment in order to reinforce their impact. They allow the pooling of resources and means: shared offices or workshops, showroom or pop-up store, knowledge, skills and know-how, access to financing and access to experts such as lawyers, accountants, designers, coaches. With an emphasis on

the collective or even an activist dimension, these spaces offer a physical work environment that is sometimes minimalist and can in some respects seem frugal, even compared to working from home.

Mixed focus: These coworking spaces propose an *à la carte* offer that tries to meet both the needs of the individual and those of the business. They take care of the attractiveness of the work environment – a major marketing ploy – while deploying an ambitious program of events and activities. Yoga or breathing classes for example alternate with training and coaching workshops (in finance, negotiation, contract law, branding, digital marketing, SEO, podcasting), community events such as breakfasts, coffee breaks or lunches (where members help each other) and inspiring events generally open to the external community, such as testimonials, round tables, networking, charity galas.

In our opinion, these rich and complex concepts are the most interesting thanks to their ability to offer a stimulating daily work environment and simultaneously involve a whole ecosystem of actors and partners around the cause of women, in turn making them visible and tangible to a wider audience. We will come back later to this aspect of thought leadership, which requires a committed and consistent editorial line.

Work collectives: the most secret ones

Members are co-opted for their entrepreneurial or non-profit project within a homogeneous work collective in a small space, shared office or workshop, from 6-8 desks and 30-40 sqm, where workstations are generally allocated. The standard subscription is monthly, but the space itself is used either full-time or part-time.

~Targets: creative women, craftswomen and solopreneurs~
🍃 *cowBonne (Barcelona), Girl Crush (Oslo), L'Atelier Viking (Nantes), La Patronnerie (Paris), Women Co (Dublin), [F]empower Stuttgart, The Tribe (Totnes)*

Clubs: the most publicized ones

Close to Anglo-Saxon clubhouses, they grant an annual membership upon application. According to some testimonials, members go there mainly for events because the space, although luxurious, is quickly noisy and therefore not very conducive to deep work.

~Targets: businesswomen and women entrepreneurs~
🍃 *The Wing & The Allbright (London)*

Parent-friendly or "cobaby": the most pragmatic ones

Founded by women confronted with the delicate equation of balancing career and maternity, these spaces offer a day nursery or childcare service to meet the specific needs of young working parents. They are popular with young mothers, who represent 60% to 80% of their members.

Their pragmatic approach also reflects a sense of activism in favor of a better recognition of maternity rights in the workplace and greater involvement of working dads at home (paternity leave, task sharing).

Through its recruitment, *Cuckooznest* also advocates the revaluation of the nanny profession through three levers: qualification, remuneration and masculinization (with "mannies" offering children male role models associated with care).

~Targets: young parents who are either working or on parental leave~
🍃 *Cuckooznest (London), Tadah (Zurich), Jugglehub (Berlin), Qf (Milan)*

Women-only: the most influential ones

Coworking spaces exclusively for women adopt a radical stance: removing the male factor from the daily work environment. Men cannot become members but are often welcome at events open to the public, unless contraindicated by the subject matter (discussion groups, non-mixed workshops, etc.). With a marked predilection for unallocated workstations in open spaces (*hot desks*), these spaces offer both monthly subscriptions and daily passes, for the most part.

As in independent coworking spaces with a community dimension, different types of activities and events aimed at conviviality, well-being and business are arranged. At their head are excellent communicators, some of whom have become champions of the cause of women in the future of work. Thanks to their regular speaking engagements in the media and on social networks, their influence can be measured on a national scale and even beyond, for example within the *DACH Region*, which includes Germany, Austria and German-speaking Switzerland, where there has been a remarkable increase in the number of women-focused coworking spaces.

~Targets: female entrepreneurs, freelancers and self-employed, women in professional transition~
🍃 *Birdhaus (Zurich - sidebar), CoWomen (Berlin), CoWomen Heidelberg, Wonder (Berlin), SALON F (Munich), Hashtag Workmode (The Netherlands), Hera Hub (Uppsala), Doors Open Female Hub (The Hague), Girlsmode (Antwerp), Comunidad Nosotras (Madrid), W.e.Space (Copenhagen - closed)*

Women-first: the most federative ones

Conversely, "women-first" coworking spaces display strong values and a positioning that is still committed to these values without formally excluding men.
Marketing and communication are geared towards women, using phrases such as *"designed by and for women, open to all"* or *"powered by women"*, with concepts again very much embodied by their leaders. This positioning also reflects a concern for increased profitability, while avoiding cutting themselves off from male customers. Indeed, managing an independent coworking business is a low-margin activity, characterized by high fixed costs and significant churn. For medium (≥ 200 sqm) to large (≥ 500 sqm) premises, renting rooms (meeting, training) and especially private offices will improve profitability and cash flow. Applying a gender criterion is no longer relevant when it comes to accommodating students, trainees and teams of employees or volunteers. This is why women-first spaces have both average and high rates of feminization.

~Targets: female entrepreneurs, freelancers and self-employed, and mixed organizations (companies, associations, etc.). ~
🍃 *Blooming Founders (London - sidebar), WeSpace (Zurich), Loffice (Budapest), O4 Flow (Gdánsk), Mona (Paris - temporary), Bonnie & Smile (Paris)*

Another community dynamic when you surround yourself with women

As an executive in the pharmaceutical industry, I have been involved for 5 years in *PWG (Professional Women's Group)* in Zurich, including 2 as President, before buying *Birdhaus*, created by Michelle Gasparovic in 2019.

Why a women's network, a place exclusively for women? My experience has prepared me to answer because I have been constantly challenged for the past 5 years. I talked to my lawyer about it and it's as legal as a women's gym. Beware, we don't advocate isolating ourselves from the rest of the world either!

The answer is that women's behavior is completely different in a non-mixed space. The heart of the matter is to have a space where women can be themselves, speak up, ask questions, have support, be surrounded and develop friendly relationships. The community dynamic is not the same as with men.

Ana Paula Tediosi
Owner & general manager at Birdhaus (Zurich)

Diversity promoters: ecosystem drive engines

Some actors position themselves in favor of female entrepreneurship by providing meeting or work spaces – some temporary and some permanent – either directly (coworking operated by a startup incubator), or in partnership with women's networks (by co-organizing events). These initiatives aim to encourage vocations and ultimately increase gender diversity on the local entrepreneurial scene.

In Warsaw, *Brain Embassy* offers a particularly successful partnership model. This coworking space is one of the pioneers of the sector in the capital, with three sites. It hosts the **Foundation for Women's Entrepreneurship** (*Sieci Przedsiębiorczych Kobiet*) and its permanent team (7 people). The foundation thus has an office in exchange for the organization of events, such as workshops (free for female residents within the limit of a certain number of places and at a fee for external participants). This is the only example of a women's professional network hosted by a coworking space whereby they work closely together to increase diversity. *Brain Embassy* thus sees its facilitation program enriched by different types of events (workshops, training, conferences, testimonials, etc.) specifically designed to bring members of the foundation into the space and eventually recruit more women into the community.

~Target: novice or confirmed entrepreneurs~

Willa incubator (Paris), Brain Embassy (Warsaw), Das Packhaus Heumarkt (Vienna - p.44), Women Co partners (Dublin - p.31 & 66)

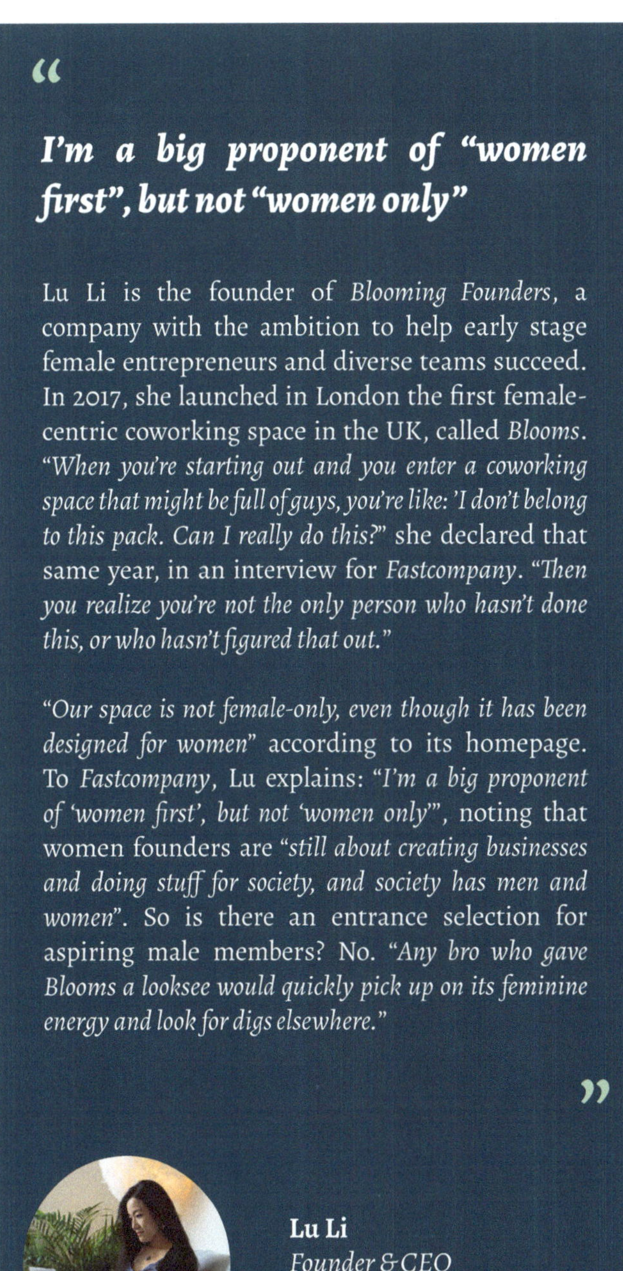

> ## I'm a big proponent of "women first", but not "women only"

Lu Li is the founder of *Blooming Founders*, a company with the ambition to help early stage female entrepreneurs and diverse teams succeed. In 2017, she launched in London the first female-centric coworking space in the UK, called *Blooms*. *"When you're starting out and you enter a coworking space that might be full of guys, you're like: 'I don't belong to this pack. Can I really do this?"* she declared that same year, in an interview for *Fastcompany*. *"Then you realize you're not the only person who hasn't done this, or who hasn't figured that out."*

"Our space is not female-only, even though it has been designed for women" according to its homepage. To *Fastcompany*, Lu explains: *"I'm a big proponent of 'women first', but not 'women only'",* noting that women founders are *"still about creating businesses and doing stuff for society, and society has men and women".* So is there an entrance selection for aspiring male members? No. *"Any bro who gave Blooms a looksee would quickly pick up on its feminine energy and look for digs elsewhere."*

Lu Li
*Founder & CEO
at Blooming Founders
(London)*

Key indicators

To complete our typology, we have selected 3 indicators in our database allowing us to compare women-focused coworking spaces and to characterize their main patterns.

2 co-founders on average

In half of the cases, the spaces have only one founder, for an average of two co-founders.

The solo founders put their personal branding at the service of highly embodied brands. They will attract, as a priority, member profiles that resemble themselves.

Nevertheless, it is by forming a duo, a trio, or even a complementary quartet (**Tadah, L'Atelier Viking**), that the founders bring together the widest range of skills – a major asset to assume the versatility required to manage a coworking space, with the necessary access to other sources of income, at least at the start.

4 types of structures, reflecting contrasting ambitions

Our sample includes 5 informal structures with no vocation to generate profits. They are either associations (some of them benefiting from subsidies or sponsorship) or groups of women entrepreneurs who share the cost of rent for the time it takes to find a viable business model.

However, the majority of coworking spaces are created for profit. Two thirds of them are businesses that are financed mainly by bootstrapping and more rarely by loans. Nevertheless, 10% are projects backed by an already profitable structure, just long enough to become profitable, such as **Wonder**, an **Amapola** project in Berlin or **O4 Flow**, an **O4 Coworking** concept in Gdánsk.

Finally, some original partnerships have given birth to temporary or itinerant coworking spaces thanks to the encounter between a community founder and a space provider (sponsor or mixed coworking).

This variety of structures reflects the challenge of economic sustainability. We will come back to this in the last section (*Inspiration*).

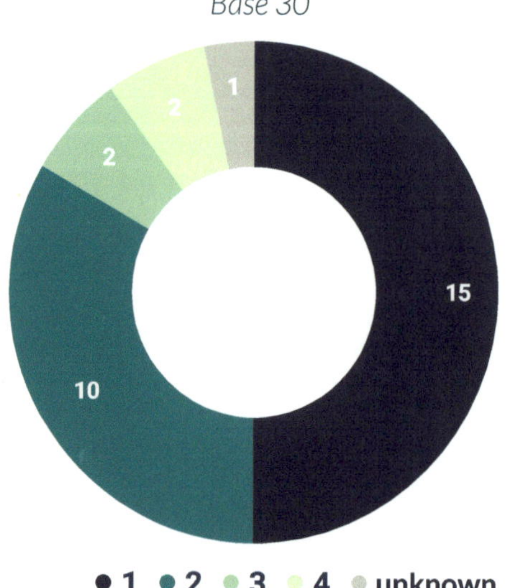

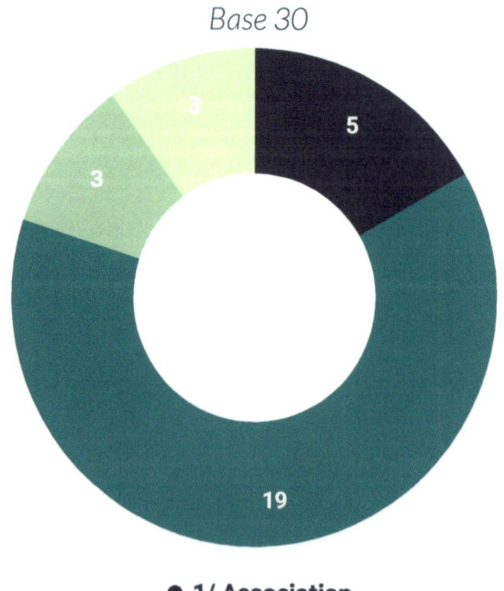

An average surface area of 214sqm
Base 28

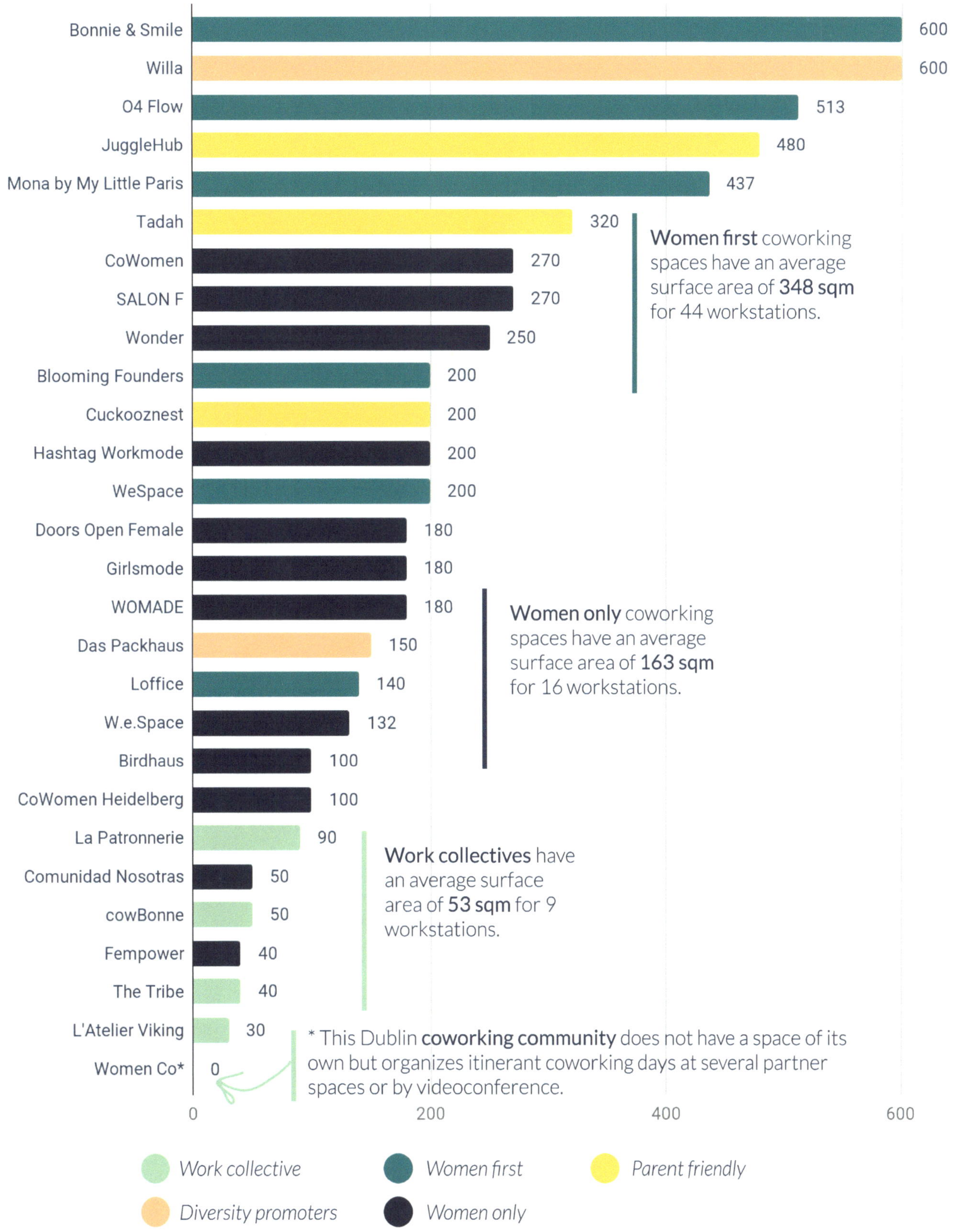

Space	Value
Bonnie & Smile	600
Willa	600
O4 Flow	513
JuggleHub	480
Mona by My Little Paris	437
Tadah	320
CoWomen	270
SALON F	270
Wonder	250
Blooming Founders	200
Cuckooznest	200
Hashtag Workmode	200
WeSpace	200
Doors Open Female	180
Girlsmode	180
WOMADE	180
Das Packhaus	150
Loffice	140
W.e.Space	132
Birdhaus	100
CoWomen Heidelberg	100
La Patronnerie	90
Comunidad Nosotras	50
cowBonne	50
Fempower	40
The Tribe	40
L'Atelier Viking	30
Women Co*	0

Women first coworking spaces have an average surface area of **348 sqm** for 44 workstations.

Women only coworking spaces have an average surface area of **163 sqm** for 16 workstations.

Work collectives have an average surface area of **53 sqm** for 9 workstations.

* This Dublin **coworking community** does not have a space of its own but organizes itinerant coworking days at several partner spaces or by videoconference.

Legend:
- Work collective
- Women first
- Parent friendly
- Diversity promoters
- Women only

Andrea Ciaramella

Alessandra Migliore

Cristina Rossi-Lamastra

Chiara Tagliaro

Note

Andrea, Alessandra and Chiara are from the Department of Architecture, Built environment and Construction Engineering (ABC) and Cristina is from the Department of Management, Economics and Industrial Engineering (DIG).

Studying gender equality in the workplace

*Research group on Workplace Management and Gender at Politecnico di Milano**

Research on gender and workplace management is scarce and scattered across multiple disciplines. This lack of conclusive and comprehensive academic research has practical consequences on the design of workplaces, and on performances and job satisfaction of workers. Four Italian scholars are pioneering this new promising research field.

Broadening the conversation

Today there is a consensus to promote gender diversity in business and organizational contexts. Scholarly conversations revolve mainly around the factors which facilitate or hamper women's career progresses.

Instead, researchers in workplace management have to date overlooked the issue of gender equality. This is rather surprising, as evidence exists that the physical and organizational features of the workplace differently affect male and female workers.

Interdisciplinary research in progress

We work on workplace management and gender at Politecnico di Milano in an interdepartmental research program. We implemented this field thanks to Alessandra's PhD research that focuses on collaborative spaces for entrepreneurship and innovation, at the crossroads of architectural design and management on one hand, economic engineering on the other hand.

Most studies available adopt a single disciplinary perspective. However, a more transversal and interdisciplinary approach allows us to identify a broader spectrum of gender-related issues in the workplace, with practical consequences on women's productivity, creativity, career advancements, leadership, status, job satisfaction, work-life balance, wellbeing, and health.

First literature review
We led a literature review on 86 academic articles published in 57 scientific journals.

Our first findings stress the urgency of the theme and its practical implications. We identified 7 types of physical and organizational features of the workplace, which researchers have recognized as having distinctive consequences on women.

We intend to expand the scope of analysis from traditional themes of workplace management (such as typology of office, perception of indoor environmental quality) to new trends, including collaborative spaces and shared facilities, which scholars define as "*commons*".

Our team is paving the way for an ambitious research agenda about gender and diversity in the future of work. ●

Immersion
The flip side of the Instagram mirror

At a time when office spaces are becoming more open, flexible and collaborative, understanding the work environment through a gender lens is necessary to ensure the full inclusion of women in the future of work. Yet the multiple motivations for women to create and join women-focused coworking spaces underline the limits of the traditional offer, designed primarily by and for men.

The value proposition of these new places is resolutely differentiated and is reflected at first glance in the choices of design, equipment, decoration and activities – choices that are promoted and staged on social networks for obvious marketing reasons. But what is at stake is much more fundamental than the addition of a *"feminine touch"* or the use of a *"girly style"* to assert a singular brand. Satisfying a female clientele is not simply a matter of replacing grey with pink, table soccer with yoga classes and after-work beer with organic wine!

Being immersive, our investigation was an opportunity to enter the flip side of the flattering, sometimes dishonest mirror of *Instagram*. This allowed me to have a practical, sensorial and subjective experience of coworking in a feminine context, as a French digital nomad, while taking the pulse of these communities. The testimonies of leaders and members reveal needs and aspirations which are specific to women and shared throughout Europe, in spite of cultural differences. However, these needs and aspirations are still largely neglected by most office spaces today.

This second section examines the motivations of the founders and members before detailing the characteristics of women-focused coworking spaces, how members make use of them and the benefits they derive from them. In summary, we offer 10 key tips for mixed coworking spaces to become women-friendly.

Photo by CoWomen (Berlin) on Unsplash.

What women want

The founders of women-focused coworking spaces have themselves had a sometimes bitter experience when it comes to the limits of the traditional workplace and (mixed) coworking spaces. They thus built their spaces based on a clear vision of what would meet their own needs, taking as a starting point their frustrations first, their aspirations second.

A coworking space of one's own

Above all, the founders point to a work environment designed by and for men. They indeed call into question spatial and physical characteristics related to the design and equipment of spaces, such as a lack of ergonomics (for example, the absence of a hook in the toilet to hang a handbag) or poor aesthetic appeal (dull colors, scattered computer cables). But what they point out first and foremost is largely immaterial and has to do with **the atmosphere of the workplace**, which is more or less welcoming, more or less benevolent, more or less studious. Our interlocutors build on a shared feeling of discomfort, psychological insecurity and even rejection. In short, a lack of inclusion.

Some founders have had this experience in the traditional workplace, during their first career as salaried employees in a company, before undertaking a reconversion towards entrepreneurship. This is the emblematic case of Hannah Dahl, co-founder of **CoWomen,** who recounts in a video how she felt when she returned from her first maternity leave, juggling between breastfeeding at home and pumping milk at the office: *"That cannot be the future of work!"* The creation of a women-focused coworking space is therefore an ideal testing ground in which to invent solutions to help achieve a new balance between professional and personal lives.

More often, however, this approach stems from the experience of a predominantly male and youthful entrepreneurial ecosystem. Above all, the startup culture encourages attitudes and behaviors that are considered inauthentic: *"acting as"* or just pretending, as the slogan *"fake it till you make it"* suggests. These injunctions generate doubts and fuel self-censorship among many people: *"Since everyone seems to be doing so well, is it normal that I have difficulties? How can I ask for help without being perceived as incompetent? Is entrepreneurship, for me, after all?"* These are common questions likely to hinder momentum, whether one is 25, 30 or 50 years old!

At the same time, women-focused coworking spaces provide **an alternative or complement to full-time home office** – not to be confused with teleworking or temporary working from home (WFH), which assumes the existence of a main workplace separate from the home. When you are a female entrepreneur or freelancer, especially in the digital world, setting up your office at home allows you to limit your fixed costs. This is the case for 75% of female self-employed in the United Kingdom for example.

But in the long run, this choice often comes at a high price: loneliness and isolation will lead either to procrastination and discouragement or to being overworked and burned out depending on one's personality. The domestic tasks of the household also add to the mental load, whether they are performed or, on the other hand, neglected. Saying *"I'm going to do the laundry"* or *"the ironing pile can wait"* while going to get a coffee is not really a break.

And contrary to still vivid representations, working at home is not a realistic option for a young mother. We discussed this with Lorena Mayer, co-founder of **[F]empower Stuttgart**, during her maternity leave. Her energetic toddler immediately invited herself into the webcam interview. Because no, a toddler doesn't spend all day napping and caring for herself on her daycare mat!

Rub shoulders with fellow female entrepreneurs

After reviewing the widely shared frustrations of the founders regarding their original or reference work environment, it is clear that they unanimously aspire to form **a community to share their entrepreneurial journey with other women**, through the highs and lows of what some describe as *"emotional roller coasters"*.

The creation of a women-focused coworking space responds to the need to exchange, share, learn, train and surround themselves with experts. It is an opportunity to meet female role models but above all **to access relevant resources – be it material, immaterial or financial – as well as specialists** fully in tune with the digital economy (lawyer, accountant, etc.). Solo entrepreneurs in particular find it difficult to find their way between traditional institutional players who are somewhat overwhelmed by digital technology and start-up support structures such as incubators and accelerators that only accept team applications in targeted tech sectors (B2B Saas, hardware, etc.).

In this respect, the Parisian incubator *Willa* is an exception in Europe. It is aimed at innovative startups (co-)founded by women who, after selection, follow a general support program. No sector is excluded, except that the jury avoids incubating two startups likely to compete directly or indirectly at the same time. These entrepreneurs are then free to establish themselves and their teams, either temporarily or permanently, in *Willa*'s mixed coworking space, which charges rates below the market average in the heart of the *Silicon Sentier* district. Finally, with its diverse program of events and workshops open to its entire community, *Willa* fosters encounters between incubated founders, coworkers, alumni and external entrepreneurs.

Nevertheless, this model *de facto* excludes freelancers and not all women entrepreneurs are in need of the prescriptive framework of an incubator, no matter how invigorating the environment may be. In her 2015 management science thesis devoted to coworking spaces for entrepreneurs, *Julie Fabbri* offers an enlightening review of the literature on this entrepreneurial support provided by incubators in the broadest sense, focused on the creation of companies and (more rarely) on their development. Some authors point to the growth of a real *"coaching industry"* where coaches are sometimes paid (salaried employees, coaches, etc.) and sometimes volunteers (mentors, tutors, etc.), deeming it difficult to evaluate its effectiveness. The French researcher then examines the collective dynamics at work between the members themselves, defining the community of practice in these terms: *"a group of people learning collectively, on the basis of frequent exchanges around their common practice, with a view to improving it and enhancing their personal activity as well as that of the other members."*

It is precisely **this logic of exchange and mutual aid between peers** that prevails in the vision of our founders of women-focused coworking spaces. It manifests itself in everyday interactions that happen in the moment: answering a question, providing a contact, sharing a tip or a good plan, resolving obstacles or blockages, etc. If it results in a business relationship, then fantastic, but it is not a goal in itself. Bartering of skills is more encouraged. At *Girlsmode* in Antwerp, for example, Yana Smits has established ten rules that new members must commit to, including mutual aid. It excludes the monetization of services between members (contrary to the primary vocation of a business network such as a *BNI group*). On the other hand, they all become ambassadors for each other, recommending one another to their clients and thus making business contributions to one another.

> ## *Our approach to business isn't 100% business-like*
>
> In *Loffice*, we naturally pay more attention to the rehabilitation of women in the workplace, and we feel that we're more sensitive to certain social issues or to art and design for example than other coworking offices. Our approach to business isn't 100% business-like.
>
> Now that we both became mothers, we experience first hand how important it is to achieve work-life balance and how an ideal working environment can help this. Besides, Coworkid is our foundation and our mission is to rehabilitate women who are going to be active again in the labour market after maternity leave.
>
> 
>
> **Panni & Kata Klementz**
> *Co-founders of Loffice*
> *(Budapest)*
>
> *Thanks to Zsófi Énekes*

In this sense, the rise of women-focused coworking spaces **fills the gaps of women's professional networks**, which are still perceived as elitist. Despite a variety of events that are considered inspiring and offer opportunities to network with women on the spot, they do not always prove to be conducive to breaking the ice and establishing fruitful links quickly. As the events are organized on a voluntary basis, the frequency of meetings is limited (monthly, bi-weekly, etc.). In the absence of premises of their own, the location and times of meetings tend to fluctuate. In spite of their efforts to renew themselves and address new generations, the well-established networks reflect the sociology of their founders: influential businesswomen and executives. As it turns out, they don't cater to the specific needs of female entrepreneurs and freelancers – whatever their age or profile – as evidenced by the proliferation of informal community self-help groups on social networks such as *Facebook*. The reason we speak of an entrepreneurial ecosystem and not a network is to deliberately focus on this very concrete, nourishing and virtuous dimension that can make a difference in the daily life of a female entrepreneur. With clear objectives in mind, they want to concentrate on the accomplishment of their tasks, in practice, very concretely, without wasting time, as Emilie Sobels' brand in the Netherlands sums it up so well: *#Workmode.* ●

Willa, incubator and "diversity accelerator" (Paris)

Women Co organizes online or itinerant coworking sessions across Dublin.

Versatile talents

Managers of women-focused coworking spaces have a remarkable track record: lawyer, former consultant at *McKinsey*, freelance make-up artist, pharmaceutical executive, IT expert, sociologist, filmmaker, yoga teacher, prospector, fashionista, financier, translator, urban planner, former school director, novelist, slasher, blogger and copywriter specialized in interior design and decoration, digital marketing consultant, psychologist, doctoral thesis researcher, etc. – the list is not exhaustive. It is impossible to draw a typical profile, and for good reason, the independent coworking sector is accessible without any condition of diploma or training. And if age and family situation play a role, it is mainly the case in the creation of coworking spaces with daycare or a nursery, by women in their thirties.

To us, one common trait stands out: these digital women are all excellent communicators. As professionals in the fields of branding, marketing, image or words, some of them put their talents to good use, even if it means keeping and developing their activity in parallel with coworking management, like **CoWomen** cofounder Kat Brendel, now a full-time podcast strategist & coach. Others take the opportunity to share their vision through a blog or a book, such as *Babe, you got this* by Emilie Sobels (**#Workmode**) or the excellent collection of letters by Lu Li (**Blooming Founders**) *Dear female founder: 66 Letters of Advice from Women Entrepreneurs Who Have Made $1 Billion in Revenue.*

Cosmopolitan cocktail

Finally, in 30% of the areas in our sample, the CEO or at least one member of the management team is of foreign nationality (sometimes with dual nationality). This finding is fairly consistent with the metropolitan geography of female coworking spaces. Perhaps is it also a sign of an ambition without borders? ●

3 questions to
Alessandra Migliore

PhD Candidate, Researcher on Collaborative Spaces & Consultant at Real Estate Center (REC), Alessandra works in the Research group on Workplace Management and Gender at Politecnico di Milano. We seized the opportunity to interview her after her communication at the 4th RGCS symposium (23rd-24th January 2020, Lyon), in order to go deeper into some intriguing points.

In your communication you mentioned a recent study by Jones Lang LaSalle (Puybaraud, 2017) which finds a significant difference between men and women in the use of "third places" (i.e. cafés, libraries or co-working spaces) at work. It results that men work from third places more frequently than women. How can we explain this difference?

AM: According to seminal Oldenburg's book *The great good place*, by "third places", we intend multiple categories of places such as cafés, public libraries, co-working spaces, etc. These spaces provide their users an informal atmosphere based on conversations and social relations, where to build a strong sense of community.

However some questions arise: To what extent does this community really exist? Is it perceived safe by women? Some studies suggest that the perceived risk of conflict in collaborative spaces or activities can challenge women workers. Moreover, while the idea of community is over-used for marketing purposes, in reality many coworking spaces assemble men and women who work side by side, but individually. Thus, women may prefer a safe and well known community of workers rather than an unknown third place.

The same study reveals that more men than women believe that the workplace impacts the effectiveness of their work. The figure is: 51% agree that their workspace allows them to work very effectively, Men (53%) more than women (50%). Is a 3 points difference scientifically significant?

AM: The study by *JLL* also reveals that workers relate effectiveness at work with the possibility to work in alternative workplaces (home, client offices or third places). Therefore, yes, 3 points in difference is a small sign that men feel on average more supported by their workspace.

This seems to reflect the usual tendency of men to show higher self-esteem and to take more confidently pride in their accomplishments. More research is necessary to dig into this first evidence. For instance, women being on average less satisfied than men both with their mainstream workplace and with their alternative third place, it is important to find out what women really want.

According to Deskmag Global Coworking Survey (2019), only 38% of coworking spaces are led by a female owner or founder. Do you agree to say that there is an issue of gender equality in the industry itself?

AM: On a global scale, the route to gender equality and diversity acceptance is still long. Nevertheless, 38% is a good and inspiring figure.

Women as coworking owners and founders can carry on an unprecedented transformation of the real estate sector, which is traditionally led by men. Driven by different preferences and needs, women can trigger radical changes and original solutions in the workplace management field. Coworking spaces, nowadays, demonstrate to be the privileged setting for this "revolution". ●

> "
> *Women as coworking owners and founders can carry on an unprecedented transformation of the real estate sector, which is traditionally led by men. Driven by different preferences and needs, women can trigger radical changes and original solutions in the workplace management field. Coworking spaces, nowadays, demonstrate to be the privileged setting for this "revolution".*
> "

Alessandra Migliore
Researcher at Politecnico di Milano

Mona (Paris) ®My Little Paris

Dear female coworker

In a niche market where supply creates demand, the success of concepts dedicated to women depends on the meeting between the vision of the founders and the expectations of their members, for whom it is often the first concrete experience of coworking.

From Labour to Work

The translation of *Du labeur à l'ouvrage* – the title of the book written by the French intellectual **Laëtitia Vitaud** on the future of work – characterizes the common context of the members we met in the women-focused coworking spaces across Europe. These users often find themselves at a pivotal moment in their careers and personal lives, confronted with the urgent need to reinvent themselves. Entrepreneurs and freelancers, most of them have experienced the world of *"hard work"* (*labeur*) in traditional companies, where salary and relative job security go hand in hand with hierarchy, a culture of presenteeism and loss of meaning. They have experienced an often sexist mixed office environment. They have chosen to leave it to become their own boss, embracing the values of craftsmanship that characterize *"work"* (*ouvrage*): independence, control of time and tasks, attention to the needs of the end user.

Some of them even go so far as to invent a tailor-made job: ethical fashion consultant and brand agent, coach & speaker in wealth management for women, agent of beauty influencer on Instagram, stress management trainer & soul-level career coach, to name but a few. We also met women in professional transition or in a phase of reflecting on their career – for example during their first maternity leave (another *"labour"*!) – or after just having relocated as is the case for expatriates.

Among the expatriates, there are a few employees who have opted for remote work. They work for companies with headquarters abroad. In any case, for all these women, **working at home full-time is not (or no longer) an option** (testimonial opposite). They need to get out of their homes, both to break their isolation, find sources of stimulation and give an impetus to their professional activity.

Birdhaus (Zürich)

"
Working at home is not sustainable

At *Birdhaus*, we share a zero-waste vegan lunch with Jeanne. Innovation & Marketing Manager at an SME in Auvergne, she followed her husband from France to Zurich. She negotiated to switch to full-time teleworking, but soon working from home became *"unbearable"*. After negotiating the reimbursement of her coworking expenses by her employer, she subscribed to *Birdhaus* to come every week, 1 day on average. She chooses it so as to participate in a weekly event hosted by the coworking space *"for openness, inspiration"*, on topics such as leadership and soft skills – today: communication – and takes advantage of the opportunity to stay at work before or after the event, depending on the time of day.

"

No man's land

But is there a specific attraction to reserving these places for women only? Asked about their initial motivations for coming, some of our interlocutors admit to being insensitive to this factor and put forward opportunistic arguments. Several retort *"I am not a feminist"* and its variant *"I am not a hardcore feminist"*. In Berlin, Mona, who works remotely, says she chose **Wonder** because it is close to her home (10 minutes walk). Later, she willingly acknowledges that this coworking is differentiated by its community, appreciating that its events are not mandatory.

The argument is more likely to appeal to users who have previously ventured into mixed coffee shops and coworking facilities, echoing the founders' observation that they are dull, impersonal and anonymous. Tongues are quickly loosened to tell **anecdotes about men, their way of appropriating these places and the incivilities of everyday life that sometimes arise in these spaces**. What do they blame their male coworker counterparts for? Three rather trivial things:

- They talk too loud;
- They tend to monopolize speech;
- Many neglect to wash their dishes.

Conversely, these women share with me their spontaneous love for the studious and friendly atmosphere of women-focused coworking spaces, being particularly sensitive to their neat and colorful decoration, as well as their choice of meals and small healthy snacks. They underline the role of gathering in small circles to get to know their fellow coworkers and exit anonymity – for example at workshops organized during lunch breaks (*Lunch and Learn* and its French equivalent: *la tablée*).

Customer research

While the phenomenon of female coworking is new in and of itself, coworking as a whole remains largely unknown to the general public outside of big cities, as Yana Smits, creator of **Girlsmode** in Antwerp, explains.

Project developers must therefore both educate their market and understand the specifics of local demand in order to adjust their offer. This is the advantage of going through a phase of prototyping and experimentation, involving potential users and, if relevant, locally active professional women's networks. We have listed a series of examples on the following page. ●

Tablée at l'Atelier Viking (Nantes)

Test and learn

Hold meetups

Organizing meetups allows project leaders to gain exposure, build community and demonstrate the benefits of bringing women together. When it opened, *Blooming Founders'* pilot space (*Blooms London*) had already sold 50 annual memberships through its free meetups, which convinced more than 2,500 people to join its *Facebook* group.

Experiment

Several communities were formed by organizing coworking sessions between women over a morning or a day, gradually increasing the frequency. *[F]empower Stuttgart* did this monthly and then weekly, before renting a part-time space 2 days a week to help her community grow. *Women Co*, on the other hand, continues to alternate between different partner coworking spaces in Dublin.

Co-create

In Copenhagen, Natalya Tarankova created *W.e. Space* without a business plan, by pooling her resources with another entrepreneur to rent a 132 m² business premises. She set up her beauty studio there and organized meetings called "Coffee space" from 9am to 11am every Tuesday, in the form of free workshops followed by a coworking session. In almost a year, she organized or hosted 50 workshops and events of all kinds, giving herself the opportunity to explore the needs of women entrepreneurs while learning more about community management. She then closed the space to devote 100% of her time to the development of her eyelash extension business *Copenlashes*.

Prototype

Many start in a small shared office, such as the first location of *#Workmode* in Amsterdam (11 workstations), *CoWomen* in Berlin (35 sqm nested in another coworking space) or *L'Atelier Viking* in Nantes in a former garage of 30 sqm (6 workstations). This prototyping phase allowed them to meet their early adopters and complete the founding team.

Create excitement

By limiting the duration of its coworking pop up to 3 months in 2017, *My Little Paris* adopted a strategy inspired by the luxury retail industry and welcomed more than 14,000 people at 150 events with free access. Sponsored by 4 brands (*Axa, Estée Lauder, Nike and Contrex*), the venue has since closed its doors but *Mona* remains a digital platform and community invested in promoting the cause of women.

Pivot

In Vienna, *Paradocks* values vacant properties such as *Das Packhaus Heumarkt*, which has been converted into a temporary coworking space. Two women, Margot Deerenberg and Veronika Kovacsova, host 100 startups and about 500 members, mostly men, in 7000 sqm. In 2018, they decided to dedicate 150 sqm to women entrepreneurs or self-employed women, with workstations at half price. Faced with a disappointing demand, they pivoted and made their event space available to local women's networks involved in promoting entrepreneurship and IT (*Womentor, Women & Code, Women of Vienna, Female Founders, among others*). This partnership is based on a knowledge or skill exchange in the communication and audiovisual spheres (photo shooting for example).

Look and feel immersion

The women-focused coworking spaces we visited have a certain number of common characteristics, both physically (layout, equipment, decoration, etc.) and organizationally (operation, service offer, etc.).

Stylish decoration

Bouquets of fresh flowers in Rotterdam, a giant soft sofa in Copenhagen, the scent of white jasmine in Gdánsk, fruit baskets in Zurich… What strikes you is the meticulous care and attention to comfort, with an extreme sense of detail. Given that the most common alternative to coworking is still working at home, this makes sense. Members report feeling "*right at home*".

Color harmony, shape of the furniture, choice of materials, home fragrance, teas, coffees and other snacks: all the senses come to the party. The founders express their style with a **taste that is in line with the latest trends in decoration and interior design**, whatever their budget. Functional office tables, trestles and armchairs, often in black or white, blend harmoniously with more chic and cosy pieces with a retro or Scandinavian influence, between silky velvet and golden metal, solid blond wood and colorful cushions. Some founders have even called on professional designers to create their own unique brand and give birth to true signature spaces, like *Birdhaus*, *Cuckooznest* and *The Tribe* (opposite).

What they all have in common is the **profusion of green plants**, well-summarized in Alba Pregja's promise on the eve of the inauguration of *WOMADE* in Brussels: "*urban jungle*". This is a strong differentiating marker from traditional offices. During the workshop *How female spaces are transforming the (co)working world* at the 2019 Coworking Europe Conference, *CoWomen* cofounder Kat Brendel shared an enlightening anecdote on this subject. When the lack of vegetation in the traditional office space is so acute, some German women go so far as to bring their own plants to the office!

These places could easily take up the adage "*retail is detail*", because nothing is left to chance. Many women join these coworking spaces to domicile their business there – or at least indicate the address on their business card – in order to capitalize on their brand image: the "*address effect*" is guaranteed.

This is particularly the case for professions that cater to a clientele which is itself female, or whose activity is based on face-to-face appointments: coaching, recruitment, therapy and personal care (naturopathy, massage, eyelash extensions to name but a few). Freelancers wishing to offer high-end services cannot afford to practice at home. They are therefore particularly fond of **intimate meeting rooms (2 places)**, which can be rented by the hour. And it is necessary to deploy a treasure trove of ingenuity to make these small hybrid rooms, between the office and the living room, welcoming and versatile. This need was taken into account when designing the space plan for *O4 Flow* in Gdánsk, for example. Dominika Rossa switched from classic glass walls to opaque walls to guarantee privacy, while adorning one of the walls with a silkscreen print evoking the surrounding nature. For *Comunidad Nosotras*, which was located in a former beauty salon in Madrid, all the treatment booths were converted into individual offices except one, which is still in operation.

Birdhaus in Zurich

The decoration, with its woven wicker armchairs and suspended light fixtures, exploits the exceptional volume of this 100sqm duplex to evoke, sometimes the perch, sometimes the nest. Upstairs, the wallpaper has a stylized bird motif. By acquiring this social club & workspace, Ana Paula Tediosi wanted to make it a place where the values of sustainable development, healthy lifestyle and feminine warmth are embodied. She spun the metaphor through three emblematic birds: *"the sea bird (healthy, productive), the night bird (empowered, competent) and the country bird (feminine, supported)"*.

The Tribe in Totnes

Don't be fooled by the warm and sensual colors of this rural pocket-sized coworking space (40 sqm). Standing out among the motivational posters that adorn the walls is the image of a middle finger! Stacey Sheppard not only hired a professional designer, but also approached furniture and decoration stores (*Made.com*, *Desenio*, *Blooming Artificial and House of JuJu Hats*) for free or discounted items. She took the opportunity to include affiliate links in the project article on her blog *THEdesignSHEPPARD*.

Cuckooznest in Londres

Making the space an extension of the house: such was the vision of this posh coworking space with childcare, just a few steps away from the City of London. The same electric blue color, embellished with yellow and pink, is used in both the coworking space and the nursery. The interior design is signed by a designer friend of the founders. Incidentally, the project was also her first and marked the launch of her business. We had the privilege of visiting the nursery, designed at child's height with different areas for care, development, play and rest, where we, in turn, would have been glad to take a little nap ;)

Prized equipment

Here is the list of amenities favoured by members in spaces with a certain surface area (from 180-200 sqm):

- Shower with mirror and hairdryer – two essential details neglected by some traditional coworking spaces (seen at: *Girlsmode, Blooming Founders, Willa*…);

- Telephone booths – so popular that one is quickly found to be insufficient (*Willa, Tadah*) – otherwise, a small room to isolate oneself;

- Adjustable office chairs – former employees of companies are more concerned with the ergonomics of the seats than with their aesthetics;

- Sofas (everywhere). On the other hand, pear-shaped footstools (*JuggleHub*) and other balloon seats (*Female Hub, Bonnie&Smile*) are rare;

- Adjustable standing desk (*Tadah*) - much less frequent than we expected in the *Deskmag* survey (2017), which reported a higher interest among women (17% said they use it often or permanently, compared to 12% of men);

- Failing this, a computer stand to work standing up (*Wonder*) or a high table with stools to adopt an active posture (*Girlsmode, Birdhaus, Willa, CoWomen, O4 Flow*);

- Second computer screen (*Jugglehub*).

*Created by four women from Zurich, the **Tadah** coworking space with childcare (opposite) offers an exceptional working environment. Luminous, peaceful and stimulating at the same time, it combines 320 sqm of raw materials (concrete, wood), a generous amount of plants and state-of-the-art equipment (telephone booths, adjustable standing desks, acoustic panels, creative roulette furniture). Atypical, it regularly hosts private events and photoshoots.*

Identified shortfalls

Here are the missing elements that, personally, failed to make us comfortable during our immersion:

- **lockers** of different sizes, e.g. for a large backpack;
- **siesta room** offering calm and privacy.

The need for a room for individual use is in line with the **taboo question: where to breastfeed, where to pump milk?** A handful of testimonials from self-employed mothers was enough to convince us of the glaring lack of suitable space. On this point, all women-focused coworking spaces should be parent-friendly, not only those with a nursery. No one should have to retreat to the disabled toilets for lack of better facilities!

Clear rules of engagement

The configuration of the space, whether compartmentalized or open plan, will dictate its rules. This is in order to facilitate various different uses of the space with working usually being the priority. Often, **working in silence** is de rigueur by default, especially in small spaces (less than 100sqm).

At *CoWomen* in Berlin, posters in the open space remind us to work silently with a ban on eating, to avoid chewing noises. On the other side of the door, the common room opens onto the kitchen, the sanitary facilities, a bar and a mezzanine, providing spaces for all sorts of gatherings, or simply to make a phone call. At *Jugglehub*, also in Berlin, the shared offices follow one another in succession. The first one has a green light: conversation and phone calls are allowed. The second has an orange light: short conversations are allowed. And the last one has a red light: absolute silence. This regulation allows each person to choose his or her workstation according to his or Wher activity.

But the more modular a coworking space is, the more its uses will vary, especially **when the open space is rented out** and reconfigured to host events (conferences, cocktails, workshops). Erwan Peron Kergourlay, Head of Operations at the Parisian incubator, *Willa*, is in charge of events and responsible for the day-to-day management of a mixed coworking space, the most spacious of our sample (ex-aequo with *Bonnie&Smile*) - or should we say: coworking spaces-time. On 600 sqm, there are in fact 45 workstations, partly fixed and reserved for incubated startups, partly flexible and accessible to outsiders on a monthly subscription basis, plus 5 meeting rooms and 2 lounges (more informal creativity rooms). When rented out for private functions, the open space can accommodate up to 100 people seated or 200 people standing.

Erwan explains the necessity of managing the crossover between the residents who don't have a designated office and private people who are renting the space for an event. He does this by organizing a fallback zone. He looks over the private events for the coming week in advance, specifying, in a very precise table, which spaces will be closed, when, and which meeting rooms and lounges will be made available in replacement (photo). He takes into account the time required to set up so that no one interferes with or is hindered by the handling of tables, chairs and audiovisual equipment. This good practice is common sense, but it is far from being implemented everywhere.

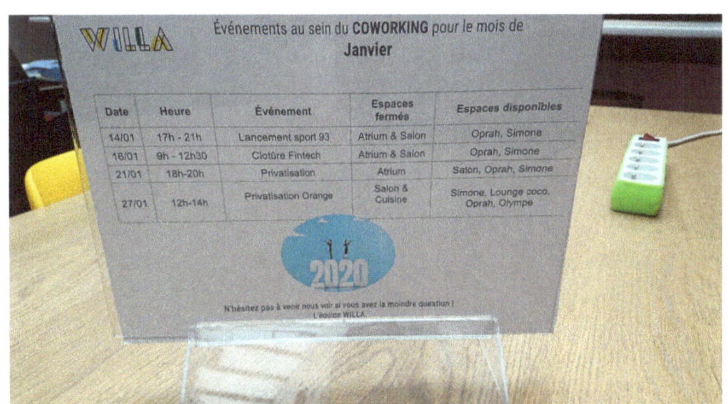

Date	Heure	Événement	Espaces fermés	Espaces disponibles
14/01	17h - 21h	Lancement sport 93	Atrium & Salon	Oprah, Simone
16/01	9h - 12h30	Clôture Fintech	Atrium & Salon	Oprah, Simone
21/01	18h-20h	Privatisation	Atrium	Salon, Oprah, Simone
27/01	12h-14h	Privatisation Orange	Salon & Cuisine	Simone, Lounge coco, Oprah, Olympe

Standing out from the crowd

Instagram asserts itself as the preferred social network of female coworking spaces and the platform has become a way for spaces to showcase their brand. They need to be "instagramable", not only to make themselves known, but for the users in turn to become their ambassadors. In short, this allows them to exist in a niche market with little media coverage.

Consequently, the layout, decoration, activities and even the complimentary consumables (food, drinks, stationary, etc.) will signal the positioning of the coworking space and become its markers of differentiation. Here are a few emblematic examples spotted during our European tour:

- **Weekly yoga classes** instead of noisy table soccer or ping pong games in the open space;

- **Varied buffet with wine & aperitif** instead of the usual beer & pizza after work;

- **Exclusively vegan shared fridge**: with this radical policy, last night's leftover bacon quiche and the bowl of tuna pasta are no longer welcome. As a result, the margin on sales is higher (snacks, meals) and a very solvent vegan clientele is flocking in;

- **Grouped delivery of healthy meals** (charged back by the coworking space) with a preference for healthy, organic, vegan, locavore or even zero waste shops and caterers using boxes or soup tureens, instead of disposable packaging;

- **Provision of beauty products** such as in hotels (soaps, creams, perfumes) and especially **new generation feminine hygiene products** (organic, transparent and ethical pads and tampons). The next step will be to normalize private sinks inside the toilets for users of menstrual cups or people undergoing hormonal injection treatment.

In this regard, several women managers are **fully assuming the showroom card**, providing benefits in kind to their users (furniture, decoration, food, complimentary consumables) while bringing in an additional income. Advertising partners seem to be very eager to reach the women who frequent high-end female coworking spaces as consumers who are well-integrated into professional women's networks – some of them real digital influencers.

Some **touches of humor** also play with the codes of startup culture and gender stereotypes:

- **Motivational poster** – we love the "What would Beyoncé do?" poster which pastiches the iconic "What would MacGyver do? poster (often illustrated with a poetic finished toilet paper roll to illustrate the concept of bootstrapping);

- **Message lightbox**, mischievously daring to reverse gender roles with *#Workmode's* 'be naked when I come home'.

- **Inclusive signage** for mixed toilet facilities with 'We ALL go to WC' at *CoWomen*, one of the few women-only coworking spaces explicitly targeting women and non-binary people on its website.

"Emergency room" at Wonder (Berlin)

- Finally, each **WiFi connection password** sends a complicit wink in the form of a mantra (altered here for obvious reasons of confidentiality): *Girlboss, Have it all, Emprender, Blooming, Flock together*, to name but a few.

Well thought-out services

In our typology (*Overview*), we highlighted the variable attention paid to the needs of the individual, the business, or a mix of both.

Even if the idea of offering a concierge service would certainly make life easier for our overworked working moms (stereotype, anyone?), there is a simple and ingenious idea that seems to hit the nail on the head. In Berlin, **Wonder** provides its members with a small 'emergency room' (photo). It is a playroom and nap room accessible on demand, where mothers can watch their children and entrust them to a coworker if they need to isolate themselves for a moment. Members use it only (very) occasionally, but feel reassured that they have a plan B (or even C) in case they cannot rely on their usual childcare arrangements.

To conclude, here is the list of the most interesting services that we have identified, in line with women's empowerment, because they highlight women as creators, entrepreneurs and thought leaders:

- **Library** specialized in personal and professional development for women;
- **Podcast recording studio** (or meeting room with optional equipment);
- **Photo shoot corner** with colorful rolls of canvas and spotlights;
- **Collaborative store** whether permanent (*Plouf* by *La Patronnerie*) or pop up (Christmas market, week of March 8th). ●

Benefits for the users

Rubbing shoulders with other women entrepreneurs not only allows members to meet up with like-minded individuals, but also to benefit from a work environment that combines emulation and solidarity. Emotional support, inclusion and a transformative experience within a sisterhood: these are the main benefits for members of women-focused coworking spaces.

Freely express one's identity

Many women report a lack of judgment and the ability to be fully oneself. Nina Helleboid, consultant and ethical fashion brand agent, member of *L'Atelier Viking* in Nantes, testifies: *"We are not here to be judged, it's not the competition of turnover, if I can help you, I help you and that's it. If the space was too much of a startup atmosphere and where we would all show-off, it wouldn't work. Here, no mask, you can be happy or in trouble, the main thing is kindness, sincerity."* Her peer, Aleksandra Jezewski, a consultant and blogger recently settled in Nantes, evokes her presence as *"an incubation in a protected psychic place"*, underlining the relevance of the attitude adopted by the founders: *"there is no pretense, no 'acting as' as can be found in coworking communities motivated by a certain type of work culture"*. But benevolence does not mean infantilization: *"this is a place where no one is going to minimize your word […] We are adults responsible for ourselves, without infantilization."* It's the very definition of a safe space.

This free and unmasked expression, which permeates the coworking spaces reserved exclusively for women (work collectives, women-only), can be found in the vision promoted by the Founder & "Connector in Chief" of the women-first coworking space, *Bonnie&Smile*, in Paris. Adeline Attia explicitly goes against what many view as the dictatorship of happiness management. Among her mottos: *"It's ok not to be ok."* Hard times and phases of discouragement are part of the entrepreneurial reality and women-focused coworking spaces prove their usefulness even more in these moments.

All moms welcome

Issues related to motherhood encounter the most benevolence in all women's coworking spaces, especially in parent-friendly spaces.

The mothers we met in the course of our investigation all point to the hostility of traditional work environments, where motherhood is seen as a hindrance – whereas fatherhood is seen as a career boost for men. The duration of maternity leave is criticized from all sides – too long it is a burden on the company, too short it is a scandalous abandonment of the young child – and then on returning to the office, breastfeeding is either encouraged or denigrated depending on the dominant culture of the country. For example, in Austria or Hungary, with maternity leave of up to 3 years, women returning to the labor market after having one or two children are considered less employable. Conversely, in London, young mothers return to work after 6 months of statutory maternity leave (up to 12 depending on the employer's policy), but the choice to return earlier or not to breastfeed is severely judged. The snag: those who choose to breastfeed do not always have dedicated space and have to improvise. And everywhere, a professional raising children will constantly be compared to the image of the perfect mother in even her slightest actions.

In London, co-founder Charlie Rosier defines **Cuckooznest** as *"a caring (non-judgmental) community of working parents"*. Her observation: an increasing number of young parents want to be (more) present during their child's early years – especially fathers – while still working. However, the traditional functioning of a crèche, which consists of dropping off the child in the morning before going to the office and picking her up in the evening, proves to be too compartmentalized. By combining a coworking space and a crèche in the same place, *Cuckooznest* offers parents more flexibility, through the possibility of going to see their children at certain times of the day. Be it for breastfeeding, playing, reading a story or sharing lunch, everyone does as he or she wishes.

In Barcelona, we interviewed Berta Calders, Event & Communications Manager, at *SocialWorkplaces.com*, host of the annual Coworking Europe conference. In February 2019, the young mother shared her outrage on *Twitter* when she was refused entry to the *World Mobile Congress* on the grounds that she was wearing her baby in a sling to breastfeed her. This was an incomprehensible rejection experienced on various other professional occasions, too. But her personal testimonial allows us to think beyond that (opposite). Berta is a member of the mixed coworking space, *Betahaus Barcelona*, where she was previously Head of Events. She details a daily organization that is divided between her home, her alternative crèche and her coworking office, all in the same neighborhood. She works part time about 20 hours a week, which she has chosen to spread over 5 days. After dropping off her child at the crèche, she goes to work at *Betahaus* from 10am to 2pm approximately, then picks her up and takes care of her for the rest of the day.

In the end, welcoming motherhood does not mean installing a crèche in every coworking space, but rather tolerating the presence of children and, most importantly, facilitating the flexible organization of each parent during the day, according to a routine that will evolve over time.

> "
>
> ## More leeway for young parents in the future of work
>
> Whether she is going back to work by choice or by economic constraint, each young mother has to face the question: how do I handle the situation? But why is the choice so divided between motherhood and career, between a stay-at-home mother model and a model of success that is ultimately very masculine? No one seems to envision an alternative! For my part, I chose to return to work part-time because it is my own definition of quality of life.
>
> Working remotely for my company, from coworking spaces, has enabled me to work part-time and simultaneously to spend time with my little one at the daycare center or at home – all in the same day. These flexibility tools and working environments should definitely empower young parents in the future of work, by crafting a satisfactory balance between their professional and private lives, in a sustainable and individual way.
>
> "

Berta Calders
Event & Communications Manager at SocialWorkplaces. com (Barcelona)

Solidarity through sisterhood

The members motivate each other to work in "focus mode" and to complete their tasks in a single sitting. Just coming in on a particular day of the week is a great remedy for procrastination and guilt about working sporadically, like a dotted line, at home. Nina, a member of *L'Atelier Viking*, explains: *"Thanks to coworking I work more, it helps me to organize myself thoroughly. By opting for Mondays I have a little more goals and ambition. It puts me on track for the week, in a much more productive state of mind, even if it means slowing down a bit at the end of the week."*

Proximity and regular contact allows members to help each other and exchange information and even **barter skills in an interpersonal manner**. This is the intention of many founders, who set up online directories of members or offer a chart organized by professions and specialties. But the one who best summarizes this approach is the founder of **W.e.Space,** Natalya Tarankova. She has transposed the spontaneous barters that commonly occur between freelancers working in beauty studios into her coworking space: *"I applied eyelash extensions in exchange for help with my accounting, my website, my social networks. You don't compare the market value of your service, you just agree between the two of you on the time to spend by each one to help the other, in a very personal way."*

This relationship, in line with the new concept of work as a craft highlighted by **Laëtitia Vitaud** in *Du labeur à l'ouvrage*, can be characterized as fellowship. Our entrepreneurs and freelancers are the creators and artisans of their (new) trade, which they learn and develop through practice. Exchanging tips, know-how and other tricks of the trade is particularly beneficial.

When it focuses on a particular project or adopts a mixed focus on both the project and the individual, events organized by coworking spaces offer complementary learning opportunities that are just as beneficial, whether it is **to ignite inspiration or to learn essential skills (entrepreneurial skills and specialized skills)**:

- Opening and inspirational events around a speaker followed by an exchange (breakfast, Lunch & Learn, *tablée*, breakfast with impulses, *Vortrag*);

- Training or coaching workshops on a rather technical or practical subject adapted to female freelancers and solopreneurs (usually in 1 hour and a half to 2 hours);

- A series of regular training programs, either on industry topics (such as *MusiCoWomen* at **CoWomen** for music professionals) or on projects (writing and publishing one's first book at **Birdhaus**);

- Monthly selection of personal and professional development books added to the coworking library based on members' suggestions and votes (also seen at **CoWomen**).

In addition, **regular weekly or bimonthly meetings** set the pace of community life and provide additional stimulation to members. Each meeting takes the form of a ritual during which each member:

- is held accountable for her activity and given a sense of responsibility (according to the principle of accountability, by sharing her progress, successes and failures from one meeting to the following one);

- becomes aware of the needs of her peers, which will act as a reflecting effect to make her aware of her own needs, and also of her strengths and resources;

- is encouraged to offer advice, suggestions and even concrete help.

Monday kick-offs and Fridays for Winners at *CoWomen* (the most ritualized model), Accountability Café (online) at *Women Co*, Mastermind at *Wonder*, and Coffee space at *W.e.Space* – these intimate encounters among women take various names and include brainstorming, co-development and troubleshooting. Their role is crucial in the development of close-knit and supportive communities of practice.

Fully expressing one's singularity, exploring at one's own pace new ways to reconcile work and motherhood, and the opportunity to evolve within a vibrant and always caring community – these benefits attested through our investigation are in line with the benefits established by research work devoted to the coworking phenomenon. These proven benefits include professional identity, emotional support and collective sense (Nathalie Mitev, François-xavier De Vaujany, Pierre Laniray, Amélie Bohas, and Julie Fabbri, 2018). However, communicating these intangible benefits – imbued with subjectivity – remains delicate, and even more so in the case of feminine coworking spaces. Many of the members that we met testify to an awareness of these benefits only after one, two or even three months following their arrival.

This is what Lu Li, Founder & CEO of *Blooming Founders* sums up perfectly: *"The experience of being in a space that is overwhelmingly female is psychologically liberating in a way few women can put their finger on until they finally experience it."* And you – will you dare to experience it? ●

the Women's Entrepreneurship Foundation team at Brain Embassy (Warsaw)

Find the right words

Cécile Strouk, writer, storyteller & host of the podcast RATURES

As a minority in mixed coworking spaces, women and non-binary people often find themselves invisibilized by a communication conjugated with a supposedly neutral male. Yet their place also depends on the use of inclusive language. Cécile tries, both in spoken and written communication, to convert minds to a more accurate use of words to make differences exist.

Coworking and mixity

I have been self-employed for 4 years and have been practicing coworking for 2 years. I left Paris for Bagnolet and swapped the nomadic posts in open space for a 2-seat office where I receive clients and partners.

In mixed coworking spaces, true mixity (the inclusion of each person as a whole self whatever his or her or their specificities) is a rare commodity: it is still very gendered and heteronormative. Probably because entrepreneurship is prized by men, even if more and more women are getting into it. Everyone seems to assume that we are heterosexual, neglecting the inclusion of lesbians, trans and non-binary people.

Beyond this atmosphere imbued with masculine codes, many elements of language conveyed by men – and women – lack accuracy. When we speak of a mixed group, to use the formula *"guys"* is to exclude the feminine, according to the famous sexist rule that we have been taught since we were little: *"the masculine prevails over the feminine".*

From inclusive writing to inclusive language

Inclusive writing in French prescribes the use of the middle point in words to include the feminine. Instead of *"experts"*, for example, write *"expert·e·s"*. Inclusive language, on the other hand, is oral. Instead of talking about *"guys"*, it is more accurate to talk about *"people"* or *"persons"* to open up the field of possibilities. For my part, I try as much as possible to use the masculine and feminine, even if it means making my sentences longer. When speaking, I prefer to use phrases such as *"les experts et les expertes"*, to refer to male and female experts. It's not easy to unlearn but, like everything else, it's a matter of habit.

In short, rethinking the place of women in mixed coworking spaces seems to me to begin with the need to profoundly modify our ways of speaking. ●

Ten tips to become women-friendly
(attention: mixed coworking spaces)

Do you want to attract and retain more members, while improving diversity in your space? Your coworking space is already dog-friendly, but have you thought about making it women-friendly? These recommendations are made for you.

#1 Zero tolerance for "bros"

Enforce the rules of etiquette. Your coworkers are your customers, not your children: it's up to each of them to do their own dishes! Also, pay attention to noise levels by distinguishing the areas dedicated to conversation and conviviality from those dedicated to concentrated work.

#2 Women-friendly by design

Taking care of the decoration is necessary but not sufficient. Pink can send a repulsive signal if it is badly dosed. Better idea: multiply green plants and invest in telephone booths to improve everyone's comfort!

#3 Pay attention to details

Take a critical look at everything that would be considered indispensable or, on the contrary, inadmissible in a home. Look, smell, touch, taste and listen so as to identify irritants. Then address them.

#4 Little corner, big impact

Toilets must be functional, smell good and have something to hang bags and coats. No woman wants to feel the difference between home and work. Also, think about menstrual cup users with at least one nice toilet with an individual sink.

#5 Break taboos

Organic hygiene product dispensers, a donation box for menstrual products, talks on the female cycle and its impact on the organization of work: the subject of menstruation (and menopause) is partof daily life in women's coworking spaces. Why not in yours?

#6 Preserved privacy

Avoid the systematic use of glass walls that turn meeting rooms into aquariums. Offer relaxation areas that promote a sense of privacy away from prying eyes.

#7 Inclusive communication

Inclusion begins with the language adopted both written and oral. It is extended in the choice of the people represented in your visuals. At events, pay attention to the diversity of the speakers as well as the fair circulation of speech among the attendees.

#8 Diversified activities

Organize events and activities aligned with the needs of your female members, who can perhaps host them themselves (yoga, fitness, public speaking). Give sufficient notice and give priority to lunch breaks, not just after-work events, so that they can easily organize themselves beforehand.

#9 Listen, listen, listen

A concept is never static and the churn of members offers frequent opportunities to consult the users. So organize targeted focus groups! If you lack parity, become a partner of local women's communities.

#10 Become allies

Learn about new approaches to diversity and inclusion (bias, stereotypes, allyship, etc.), sensitize your whole team and explore the practical implications for the activities and daily management of coworking. Speak openly about your wish for all stakeholders to contribute to this progress.

Inspiration
Pioneering spirit

There is no manual, no instructions for use. The creation of a space and the management of a female coworking community is a leap of faith. It is a plunge into the unknown and, each time, a unique adventure that can quickly turn south in the face of obstacles due to a lack of sustainability. From this point of view, the women leaders we met are all pioneers, fighting every day for acceptance, profitability and sustainability.

In this regard, the latest global survey conducted by *Deskmag* covering coworking spaces in 2019 reveals a significant difference in profitability according to the gender of the person leading them (all types of spaces considered). If the owner or founder is male, space is declared profitable in 52% of cases, at break-even in 27% of cases and in deficit in 21% of cases. But if the owner or founder is a woman, the share of profitable spaces falls to 38% (-14 points), the share of spaces in deficit rises to 31% (+10 points), and the share of spaces in equilibrium remains at a relatively similar level, at 32% (+5 points).

Even if there is still a lack of hindsight and precise figures to assess the profitability and long-term sustainability of the different models of women-focused coworking spaces, our survey highlights the best practices observed *in situ* and identifies the pitfalls that can be easily avoided. Reflecting on our own business plan, we've also shared the action levers that seem the most promising to us according to different scenarios.

In our view, the quest for a sustainable women-focused coworking model will be played out on two main fronts. First, the community front, which will be about creating, developing and maintaining customer loyalty over the long term. Second, the financial front, which is based on an effective diversification of activities and ultra rigorous management.

In this third section we reveal the good practices identified through the critical analysis of 30 coworking spaces, before addressing the specific challenges facing women-focused spaces in the coming years.

Tadah, coworking space with childcare (Zurich)

Building a community

A women-focused coworking space is only an empty and soulless shell that is doomed to fail if it does not build a committed and involved community of women entrepreneurs, freelancers, independent workers and salaried employees – in transition or otherwise. It is far from intuitive at first glance but, by reviewing various examples of prototyping and experimentation (p. 43), we have seen how relevant it is to **create a community before opening** such a space. Indeed, this is one of the key recommendations the *CoWomen* team offers in their checklist, *What it takes to open a space (for women)*: "*Start with the community first*", highlighting the opportunity to surround yourself with allies and perhaps even find co-founders, as they did in their own case.

Community management is a demanding activity that requires regular communication but also listening and interacting with members in a very personalized and empathetic way. It is a key mission assumed by (at least) one person, often the founder or a co-founder, in the early stages of creation, before being (sometimes) entrusted to a community manager or office manager, who will manage the social networks in parallel. To create and develop a community, **we recommend using the Community Canvas** (opposite). Organized in 3 sections (identity, **experience**, **structure**), it covers 17 key themes to formalize a vision and assess its implementation. The central identity section has already been covered extensively (notably in the first section, *Overview*) so we will focus here on the top section detailing the experience of members according to 7 themes, in the form of a process that goes from selection on the left (arrival) to transition on the right (departure from the community).

A framework to shape meaningful communities

Selection

The selection (or not) of members is a decisive choice that is not made everywhere in our sample. The desire for inclusion would tend to lean towards the absence of selection – which in practice translates into self-selection of the candidates. On the other hand, it is a good way to build a community with minimum homogeneity around a common mindset and shared values. Therefore, management can choose to wait one to two years before setting up a process and criteria, as *CoWomen* did this year.

🍃 *Online form, application form detailing the entrepreneurial project, sponsorship by a member, coffee with a founder, interview during a visit to the space...*

Transition

Like the selection, the departure of members deserves equal attention, as word of mouth plays a major role in the reputation of a women-focused coworking space.

A departure is not always definitive. In addition to careful communication, administrative matters such as the invoice for the cancellation of the membership or the return of the deposit must be settled quickly to leave a positive impression. The treatment of members who have become inactive must also be determined.

🍃 *Departure email, invoice, return of deposit, postcard, photo souvenir, alumnae network...*

Rules

Enacting rules concerning safety, manners, organization and what is expected from members in terms of attendance to events and cooperation, for example, is essential to create a safe space. Of course, it is necessary to share them during selection and integration, but also to ensure that they are respected. Depending on the founders' intentions, community events are more or less numerous and members' attendance is more or less recorded. In order to guarantee a sincere and spontaneous commitment from the members, the managing team has to demonstrate assertiveness while letting each member freely determine whether or not she will attend. This requires a subtle balance! On the other hand, some rules can't be compromised. In cosmopolitan metropolises like Berlin, where it is not uncommon to have discussions in three different languages on the same day, it is the lunch facilitator who will determine whether the discussion can be held in German or whether it should be switched to English due to the presence of a foreign participant whose mother tongue is not German.

🍃 *Rules of procedure, charter, welcome email, poster, video...*

Roles

In addition to rules that are meant to apply to all, different roles can be defined to involve certain members in the management of the space. A typical example: giving a key to ensuring the space is opened and the equipment (light, coffee machine, alarm, etc.) is switched on in the morning, and then locked and switched off in the evening, on one or more days a week. Other examples: welcoming visitors to present the space to them, or taking care of the plants.

This involvement makes sense for two reasons. On the one hand, it makes certain members feel responsible and that their actions are valued, which tends to increase their loyalty. On the other hand, it relieves the management team of the constraints linked to long operating hours, while lowering the operating costs of the space. The only precaution is to check questions of liability and insurance beforehand, even if it means contracting a recurring service.

🍃 *Procedure, instruction sheet, discharge, contract...*

Shared experiences

Whether it's about the design of the physical space, its operation or the events that take place there, the team must remain attentive to the way in which the members appropriate the space, the project, and its vision, and ensure the harmonious cohabitation of its members. The shared experiences cover both the overall experience within the space and the events that punctuate the life of the community at regular intervals.

Events could take the form of weekly meetings, both physical and virtual, which are particularly conducive to forging ties, developing conviviality and fostering accountability, as we have already mentioned. It is an opportunity to recall the community rules concerning the conduct, the allocation of speaking time and mutual aid among members. As the year progresses, other important events can be added (back-to-school, Christmas, 8th of March, etc.) and lead to committed initiatives (solidarity collection, clothing swap, ephemeral store, to name but a few).

🍃 *Mondays kick-offs & Fridays for Winners (CoWomen), Accountability Café (Women Co), Mastermind (Wonder), Coffee space (W.e.Space), brainstorming (Doors Open Female Hub)...*

Rituals

In addition to shared experiences, rituals enable members to align with the community's objectives and values. Rituals also symbolically mark members' integration into the community, for example, by hanging their photo on the wall, announcing their arrival in an internal newsletter, offering them the opportunity to introduce themselves at the beginning of an event or offering them a gift.

🍃 *Breakfasts, lunches, Tablées (L'Atelier Viking), Vegan Lunch (Birdhaus), Vortrag ([F]empower Stuttgart), group selfie at the end of each meeting (Women Co)...*

Content

The challenge is to create content that provides real value for members. It is therefore necessary to ensure the relevance, consistency and renewal of topics from an editorial point of view, whether through a newsletter, a blog, a video channel, a podcast or events. This is not an easy task in metropolitan areas that are sometimes already saturated with numerous free meetups, many of which – particularly in recent years – cater to communities of female entrepreneurs.

In this regard, does a vegan chocolate cake workshop really have a place in a women-focused coworking space? We doubt it – unless it is an initiative proposed by a member who is about to publish a recipe book or launch her catering business! Based on the community newsletters we studied, our preference tends toward subjects of inspiration and empowerment that remain largely unknown or taboo, such as work organization and menstrual cycle, balancing one's hormones naturally or, even more mysteriously: a lunar circle! ●

The people who choose you create your community

Through my research and prospective firm, I have gradually identified the specific expectations of women and the Millennial generation towards the future of work by 2030.

But it is above all by experimenting various spaces in Paris with my team that I became aware of how masculine the codes and actors of coworking were. In creating *Bonnie&Smile*, I made the bet of an inclusive place – thought and animated by women but open to all – and chose to welcome residents unconditionally. I meet them individually for 1 hour to learn about their professional and personal needs, and then connect them. I put forward a very embodied concept, often offbeat. One morning, I offered a pair of slippers to a resident to take him at his word after a discussion!

The good surprise? The people who choose you create your community. Those who don't adhere to the concept step aside on their own. As a result, the only people that remain are the fans, who actively participate in the animation and bring ideas, acting as true ambassadors. The capacity to train men is then very strong. And I find it exhilarating to see the exemplarity of women!

Adeline Attia
*CEO & Connector in Chief
at Bonnie&Smile (Paris)*

Making a profit

As with any business, but even more so in a low-margin activity, the sustainability of a women-focused coworking space relies on a solid business model. From the outset, project leaders must adopt a state of mind that is not only activist and user-centric but also resolutely business- and productivity-oriented. The economic equation is complex, quickly dismissing those who would see it as a form of lifestyle entrepreneurship, neglecting the fundamentals of the business and financial management.

Our web research has indeed enabled us to identify a certain number of projects that were aborted or closed down after a few months, a year, or two years at the most, and could not be included in our study sample (with one exception). However, according to the *Deskmag* global survey (2019), coworking spaces take an average of 3 years to break even. So here are the 4 main action levers identified at the end of our study.

Lever #1: Balancing the business model

By default, a coworking space already encompasses at least three types of activities:

- provision of dedicated or flexible workstations in an open space or in a closed office, either via a daily pass or a monthly subscription;
- rental of meeting rooms;
- renting out the space or part of the space for private events.

Achieving profitability based on this triptych is possible, despite a very competitive market and seasonal fluctuations in activities. This is first and foremost thanks to the income stream brought in by renting out meeting rooms and the space as a whole. To achieve this, it is necessary to dedicate a salesperson to business development.

Above and beyond the typical streams of income, our study highlights 3 additional scenarios of creation and development in the attempt to break even.

Scenario #1: Coworking as an extension of the mission

In this scenario, the founders are already running a profitable business, such as: a training center (*Female Hub*), a digital marketing agency (*Comunidad Nosotras*), a research and prospective firm (*Bonnie&Smile*), or a beauty studio (*W.e.Space)*. The creation of a coworking space is then considered as a complementary activity, as an extension or even a spin-off of the original mission. Some go as far as to see it as a marketing expense in order to develop and diversify their pre-existing clientele, as it is also a powerful advertising tool.

The interest of this scenario is to capitalize on rent that has already been paid or to consider that coworking must generate just enough revenue to cover the additional cost of choosing a slightly larger space. However, managers must structure and manage their team in such a way as to clearly allocate responsibilities and delegate day-to-day management as much as possible.

Scenario #2: Coworking as a starting point for diversification

In this scenario, the coworking space is a starting point for diversification, either with the core target clientele (the members), or with a corporate clientele, which is more interesting financially but with a significantly longer business development cycle. Even if there are many diversification possibilities, they must be part of a well-thought-out strategy in order to avoid dispersion and to maintain coherent and credible communication toward stakeholders.

🐦 Diversification based on the physical space

While an intimate and suitably equipped open space is favored by the creators to stimulate exchanges and meetings (and optimize the number of sqm per workstation), the **rental of private offices** for small teams ensures higher revenue and better opportunities for recurring cash flow. Otherwise, a team hosted in an open space can quickly become invasive and undermine the overall community dynamic. The alternate rental of such private offices to several different teams on different days of the week is already a reality (seen at *Blooming Founder*) but the increased use of teleworking since the Covid-19 pandemic could accelerate this trend. It is up to the women-focused coworking spaces to comply with the reinforced hygiene protocols that need to be implemented

during the rotation of the teams. Another rental segment also caught our attention: **intimate meeting rooms** (2 places) for which the overall market offer seems lacking. These can be rented out by the hour to professionals in coaching, recruitment, therapy and personal care. We have observed several coworking spaces that did this as a means to utilize a small office or split up a larger meeting room with insufficient occupancy. The benefits are twofold. On the one hand, the demand is very solvent: clients will book the space for sessions that they have already sold themselves. On the other hand, they introduce the venue to potential future members.

In addition, various **concierge services**, such as the sale of meals and snacks (especially the zero-waste vegan dishes already mentioned) increase the income per member. Finally, some coworking spaces develop **merchandise** around their brand (T-shirts, mugs, accessories, stationery). However, the most interesting margin seems to come from **partnerships with advertisers** through product launches, showrooms, pop-up stores, etc.

🐦 Diversification based on the skills of the team and the community

A women-focused coworking space offers a prime setting for offering **training programs and B2B or sector-specific coaching services**. Examples include *Doors Open Female Hub* (with training courses or seminars in management, leadership, etc.) and *Birdhaus* (writing cycle). Several spaces intend to develop directories of experts accessible at negotiated rates for their members, which might also be made accessible externally through a subscription. It is with sector-specific coworking and networking programs that *CoWomen* stands out, having for instance created *MusiCoWomen* for women in the music sector.

🐦 Diversification based on the development of a new area of expertise

Just as members learn and develop new skills by frequenting the community, over time the leaders of women-focused coworking spaces develop a vision, convictions and innovative tools, which give them (or reinforce) unique know-how on topics of leadership, entrepreneurship, management, diversity and inclusion. In this respect, a good example is *CoWomen*'s consulting services, *Making Business Female*, which is aimed at companies wishing to attract and retain female talent and fully unleash their potential.

Scenario #3: Coworking as the embodiment of a community

In this scenario, the community precedes the creation of the place, sometimes by several years – the time to create sufficient demand to guarantee the rapid rental of a significant number of workstations upon inauguration. This cautious strategy makes it possible to refine the concept and deal with a certain number of objections from financial partners of the project, while at the same time initiating a community dynamic as soon as the location is opened.

As an example, Dominika Rossa, Head of Women in the *O4* coworking space in Gdánsk, created a community of women more than a year before the opening of *O4 Flow* at the end of 2019. As for *Tadah* in Zurich, the creation of the digital magazine and community dates back to 2016, the time for the 4 co-founders to set up their coworking crèche. This last business model is the most perilous because both coworking and crèche are low-margin businesses, making cross-financing impossible. *Tadah* is therefore putting a considerable amount of effort into ensuring enough meeting room rentals and private events. To their favor, they have one major asset: a thorough prior knowledge of advertisers in the early childhood and parenting market.

Conversely, a coworking community such as **Women Co** in Dublin does not necessarily have the intention to open a space as rental rates in the Irish capital are very expensive. However, Magda Kuraczowska, co-leader of the community and also an ambassador for diversity in business, shared with us an original concept based on the principle that women should feel welcome and comfortable wherever they go. She believes their varied needs call for equally varied options, not just coworking spaces that are exclusively reserved for them. Therefore, she hosts community coworking days alternately in several partner spaces, thereby contributing to a greater awareness of the inclusion of women among the leaders and members of mixed coworking facilities. The arrival of a group of fifteen women is rarely unnoticed. Sensational!

Scenario #4: Coworking as a network or franchise?

There is a fourth scenario, regularly cited by creators of women-focused coworking spaces during their first year of operation, but which our study was unable to confirm.

It consists of developing a network of coworking spaces, either owned or franchised, based on the initial concept. The economic model of "independent" women's coworking spaces, which is not always stabilized, proves to be difficult to scale-up. In this respect, **Birdhaus** owner Ana Paula Tediosi believes it is risky to duplicate a community. Will what worked in one town work elsewhere? The answer is unclear, at least to the point of envisaging a franchise model, the workload of which should not be underestimated either (standardization of processes, contractualization, training of franchisees, etc.). Moreover, in crossing European borders, a coworking concept will probably come up against cultural differences. As the licensee of the American **Hera Hub** brand for Sweden, Sophia Renemar participates from Uppsala in the weekly video conferences organized for American franchisees and sees how much the realities already diverge between states and regions within the United States!

In the end, **#Workmode** represents an exception with its 5 spaces spread throughout the Netherlands. Organized around a tightly knit team, the network is nevertheless confined within national borders. Emilie Sobels' strategy has been particularly agile, at the rate of one or two openings per year between 2015 and 2018, with a focus on rather small spaces. At the location we visited, in Rotterdam, various members take on the ("basic") office management duties and (day-to-day) community management tasks, either on a voluntary basis or in return for payment.

Lever #2: Ensuring member loyalty

The quality of service provided to members is key in building their loyalty. You have to get up every morning to give your best and face all kinds of requests without being reluctant to do so. Suzanne Mau-Asam, founder of *Doors Open Female Hub* in The Hague, says: *"The learning curve is very stiff! Because the feedback loop is very short. If there is a request or a problem, you have to solve it straight away. It is intense."*

Then you have to retain the solo entrepreneurs, keeping in mind that the most ambitious ones have the intention to develop their company by recruiting a team, and will eventually leave for bigger premises. Loyalty over time is the best argument for recruiting new members because a brand, however strong it may be on social networks, will never convince members to join better than through evidence. Loyal members make the best ambassadors: recommendation as well as word of mouth are the best acquisition channels.

Member retention also goes hand in hand with the **development of subscriptions**, which improves retention and increases revenue recurrence at the same time. But almost everywhere, the question of membership formulas, and especially their price, is proving to be a thorny issue. Very regularly, however, the rates charged for women are already in the low range or even lower than local market prices, particularly in cities where coworking is most developed (Paris, London, Berlin, Warsaw). This is to such an extent that one may wonder about a perhaps counterproductive effect: what value should be placed on the service that is being sold off? In her manual *You're not broke, you're pre-rich*, *Vestpod* CEO and founder *Emilie Bellet* reveals a particularly interesting additional factor, drawing on Thomas Gilovich's research in psychology. In the short term, buying a consumer product activates a reward circuit in the brain, so we naturally tend to spend money on material goods rather than on experiences even though these very experiences are proven to contribute most to long-term happiness. However, according to another researcher, Ryan Howell, although people are well aware of this, they continue to buy material goods because they think they represent better value.

Paradoxically, women would be responsible for 75% of household expenses but, as entrepreneurs, would be unable to invest in their work environment – and their

success – by subscribing to a women-focused coworking space. This statement is deliberately provocative, but as far as we know, no one so far has managed to put a figure on the gains received by using women-focused (or other) coworking spaces, particularly when considering a return on investment. Difficult to calculate, this amount would imply taking a sample and, over a sufficient period of time, measuring the turnover generated by connections, recommendations, business contributions and services provided between members. Also to be factored in would be the simultaneous savings made on training and other services included in the membership fee if they were purchased individually.

In any case, a **refined sales pitch** is necessary to sell more and better subscriptions. Here are some good practices in this area:

- Offer full-time and part-time subscriptions, as the target customer often prefers, at least initially, a formula equivalent to 1 to 2 days per week (i.e. 4 to 8 days per month), which proves to be much more accessible financially (approximately €150 to €200 at the bottom of the range);

- Do not communicate the total cost of the subscription per year (which can be frightening) but rather per month, specifying the cost per day according to the formula (which is, in fact, not so expensive);

- Do not offer hourly access like a coworking café or a subscription in the form of a package of hours, let alone with a badge that counts down the time spent to the minute: after only a few months, *Tadah* deactivated this system, which encouraged some members to split their membership into multiple short stays, sometimes as short as 1 hour or 1 hour and half, making attendance unpredictable and unmanageable, while limiting the spontaneous creation of informal links between members;

- Where appropriate, test a less expensive daily pass rate corresponding to the price of a half-day – closer to the actual length of time that some users are present as they alternate with outside appointments. However, this pass does not allow for participation in community

events, following the example of *Birdhaus*, which immediately compensated for the loss of margin through an increased occupancy rate;

- Completely prohibit free passes (even for a trial day) because it costs you with no impact on your sales (by attracting the least solvent people, off-target) while annoying your community;

- Involve members in the daily management and animation of the space to limit fixed costs and guarantee controlled rates.

In terms of management, it may also be interesting to offer subscriptions at preferential rates in return for a half-year or one-year commitment, or general terms and conditions of sale requiring 30 days' notice in the event of termination in order to limit cash flow fluctuations. Reflect on how relevant it is to require a deposit at the subscription of a membership, as this expense has a definite impact on the clients' finances and discourages those who have just launched their business.

Finally, to avoid the "stop and go" phenomenon consisting in suspending one's monthly subscription during the summer vacations or even every other month to "save money without losing contact with the community" (an authentic anecdote), we have noted a mixed coworking space which required a waiting period of 3 months before allowing a return to a subscription (except that this community coworking space was operating at its full capacity and offered full-time monthly memberships only).

Suzanne Mau-Asam (in black) at Doors Open Female Hub (TheHague) photo by Kim Verkade, Creative Imagine.

Lever #3: Optimizing the occupancy rate

If only one key performance indicator were to be retained, it would be the occupation rate of work stations, which must be the obsession of managers on a daily basis. We list 5 good practices that are probably common sense for many, but the culture of yield management is unevenly distributed among female coworking leaders.

To determine the size of the space, we must first take into account the location, which affects accessibility and allows us to define the catchment area. Indeed, travel time influences the frequency with which members will come during the week: potentially every day if they live 10, 15 or at most 20 minutes away, as opposed to only 1 to 2 days if they live 20-30 minutes away (not much more). In the wake of the Covid-19 epidemic, the *European Coworking Assembly* cites the concept of *15 minutes city* (Carlos Moreno) as a structuring trend for the coworking industry, particularly in rural and suburban areas.

We found a sometimes disappointing occupancy rate in medium to large coworking spaces, even in good locations, because members were looking for flexibility and flocked unpredictably or depending on the weather! There were almost as many subscribing members as there were available workstations... except that the majority had subscribed part-time memberships! In this case, on the contrary, you have to sell 2 subscriptions per workstation (at least) and transparently apply the principle of "first come, first served" as is the case at *Wonder* in Berlin. Each person takes the necessary steps to arrange themselves accordingly.

Smaller spaces, on the other hand, boast the best occupancy rates, which soar to 100% while avoiding overbooking. How do you do it? It is in Nantes, in *L'Atelier Viking*, the smallest women-focused coworking space in Europe of the collective work type, that we discover the most accomplished system: subscriptions are offered part-time for a modest budget, with a workstation assigned on one (or two) fixed day(s) during the week, which cannot be used in case of absence. To encourage the rapid weaving of a community, the days have been opened progressively: first only on Mondays and/or Tuesdays, then on Wednesdays, and finally on Thursdays, knowing that Friday is reserved for private events. The result: 30 members for 6 workstations in 30sqm.

And in Paris, *La Patronnerie* operates on an identical model with 10 workstations, keeping one available to serve as an adjustment variable and guarantee the flexibility of access so dear to our women entrepreneurs.

Finally, here are some other ways to boost the occupancy rate:

- Organize events during lunch break, with the effect of boosting the attendance of the place on the same day;

- Sell trial day passes on off-peak dates, like **Doors Open Female Hub**, via *Eventbrite* or as a pack on the day of an event (conference or workshop + half-day coworking).

Last tips

The quest for profitability requires managers to be on all fronts at the same time, demonstrating incredible versatility, especially since, in the case of the solo founders, we haven't met any who don't have a dual function. For optimized space management, the search for productivity and the implementation of automated procedures must start as soon as possible, because when the activity takes off, there will often not be a moment left to redesign the processes.

When it comes to the organization of the leader, the basic reflex is to compartmentalize her activities as much as possible by practicing:

- Timeboxing (the opposite of multitasking to be fast);

- Planning days (or half-days) dedicated to such and such an activity over the week to avoid zapping systematically;

- Filtering incoming requests (phone calls, emails, forms, complaints) and automating appointment scheduling in the agenda for all recurring requests such as visits, calls, press requests, etc.

As far as tools are concerned, the technologies are there, the market is mature, and we might as well use them right away. Market leaders such as *Nexudus, Cobot* or *Andcards* are commonly used within our sample and prove to be relevant in the case of meeting room rental (to manage both time credits included in subscriptions and reservations from outside). Otherwise, the combination of tools adapted for invoicing subscriptions and events, as well as the digital marketing funnel do the job perfectly, with for example *Hubspot, Eventbrite* and *Mailchimp* combined together. You might as well sharpen your digital tools and go into battle armed! ●

Mona

Facing new challenges

Other challenges await women-focused coworking spaces as well. Just as our European tour reveals how much the market remains to be educated and the visibility of women-focused coworking spaces deserves to be reinforced, the coworking sector is in turmoil, navigating both the economic crisis and new needs linked to the growth of teleworking, while still astounded by the resounding fall of the giant *WeWork* and in the process of commoditization through the concept of Workspace as a Service (WaaS). Faced with a service that is becoming commonplace, the very name *"coworking"* is becoming so controversial that it is being debated, if not rejected outright by some of our stakeholders in favor of the terms *"platform"*, *"co-learning"*, *"hub"*, *"social club & workspace"* and *"community"*. All in all, the landscape is far from gaining visibility!

Concerning the sustainability of the business models, the relationship of women to money and the solvency of clients remains a burning subject, even more so with the greater impact of the economic crisis linked to Covid-19 on women. On average, women are expected to be more affected than men by this crisis, which affects the service industry more so than compared to the previous crises which affected mostly the financial market and/or the industry. Will the economic conjuncture discourage the opening of new places or will it accelerate them as a response to the emergence of new female vocations in the way of entrepreneurship and freelancing, in the wake of these crises? The inauguration of **WOMADE** in Brussels this year, finally postponed from spring to autumn by Alba Pregja, makes us lean towards the second hypothesis.

In terms of positioning, the personal branding of the founding team plays a key role in embodying the coworking brand image and reaching its audience. The choice must then be made between having different generations cohabit the space or maintaining a strong homogeneity by identifying with the CEO or the values she embodies. We were disappointed and shocked to hear some inappropriate phrases tinged with ageism during one of our interviews. In this respect, intergenerational cohabitation can quickly dispel prejudices about the impact of age on women's digital dexterity – prejudices induced by the caricatured representation of generations X, Y, and Z. On the other hand, it will be more delicate to create consensus around a shared vision of feminism, whose approaches and conceptions are, to say the least, contrasted, depending on the identity and personal situation of the members. For now, age is a strong marker, with younger members adhering to a feminism that is more action-oriented than their elders.

However, our greatest disappointment lies in the **relative lack of cultural, social and ethnic diversity of these women's communities**. Entrepreneurship and freelancing present fewer and fewer barriers to entry but seem reserved for certain socio-professional profiles. Ethnic diversity remains a subject that is still taboo or poorly measured, while a shudder of impatience can be observed in light of the *#Blacklivesmatter* movement. Whether we love it or hate it, the American brand *The Wing* struck people's minds with its clearly communicated biases in favor of women of color (black and Latinas) as well as LGBTQIA+ people (at least before the scandal broke out about their controversial management practices). Faced with the prospect of seeing *The Wing* settling in Paris or the inner suburbs one day, a black Parisian woman confided to us: *"People like me are looking forward to it."* Defending a fairer place for women in the future of work is therefore part of the necessary fight against racial discrimination and recognition of the specific realities experienced by women of color in a so-called *"intersectional"* perspective.

Independent coworking spaces have long been aware of this issue, as *Bernie J Mitchell* (opposite) testifies. However, it is now on the agenda to put in place concrete measures to increase diversity and is the subject of a committee at the *European Coworking Assembly* under the aegis of two women, the President *Jeannine Van der Linden*, Founder and Manager of *De Kamer*, a network of collaborative coworking spaces in the Netherlands, and the Director of Diversity, Equality & Inclusion *Tash Thomas*, who is a LGBTQ+ Activist in the UK. We could make similar considerations about the inclusion of people with disabilities, noting that only one women-focused coworking founder in Europe publicly mentions her invisible handicap, but not in the advertising of her space, only in an interview found online. In terms of inclusion, will women in their turn be exemplary? ●

You can be welcome without feeling invited.

The issue of diversity has been slow to emerge in the world of independent coworking. It led to the organization of events for several years without achieving a real federation of will. Until this article published by *Alex Ahom* on Medium in November 2018 entitled *The business case for diversity in your workplace*, which finally reached its audience in the wake of the 2018 edition of the sector's event, *Coworking Europe Conference*.

Awareness is now growing in the United States, with *Black Bird* Coworking for African-American women, for example, or here in London through initiatives aimed at our ethnic minorities, the *BAME (Black, Asian & Minority Ethnic)*.

In the podcast that I co-host within the association *European Coworking Assembly* I was marked by the fight of *Kofi Oppong*, founder of *Urban MBA*, involved here in inclusion through sport and entrepreneurship. He explains that among young people, people from minorities do not really feel invited to take part in new ways of working and to join the coworking movement. But this story can and must change by highlighting more role models and ensuring a fairer and more equitable representation of this talented youth!

Bernie J Mitchell
Coworking marketing & strategy consultant (London)

WomenCo (Dublin)

Conclusion

Empowered women shaping another future of work

Our investigation reveals a booming movement throughout the entire European continent. Reflecting the diversity of their creators and members, women-focused coworking spaces present multiple faces. Their study does not reveal a specifically European model, but rather a rich landscape composed of six model types – parent-friendly, clubs, women-first, women-only, work collectives & diversity promoters – drawing a landscape of great richness.

Because many are still looking for a profitable business model in a low-margin coworking sector now hard hit by the Covid-19 crisis, these specific coworking spaces remain fragile. But isn't this the lot of all concrete utopias? The founders' tenacious quest for acceptability, profitability and sustainability, made up of intuitions and doubts, trials and errors, is as challenging as it is admirable. Warriors and craftswomen: let's pay them the tribute they deserve here!

Gradually abandoning the protective and emancipating luxury of a private room once so precious to Virginia Woolf, these women are shaping, in their own way, places of empowerment that are now collective, allowing women not only to see but above all to live the concrete and sensitive experience of new forms of sisterhood. It is a question of conquering a new horizon of opportunities: the future of work. It is a contribution to shaping a fairer place for women and non-binary people. In response to the dystopia depicted by Emily Chang with *Brotopia*, these communities prefigure the advent of a new era that we will call: *Sistopia*.

Controversial, female coworking spaces astound and detonate. They challenge the status quo, forge new representations, encourage new vocations, stimulate the development of new talents and impel a radical change in mentalities. Even if they do not escape the challenge of cultural, social and ethnic diversity posed to the entire coworking sector, they are the crucibles of an inclusive future of work, which harmoniously combines masculine, feminine and, why not, neutral.

It's up to us to draw inspiration from them and make their voices heard in the public debate and the media!

Ivanne Poussier
CEO & Co-Founder
Ada Coworking

Sources

Market research

DESKMAG. Global coworking survey (2017, 2018, 2019).

Infuture Institute, *Coworking. I want it that way*. Gdánsk, 2019. http://infuture.institute/raporty/coworking-i-want-it-that-way

Academic research

BLANCHARD, Soline, BONI-LE GOFF Isabel & RABIER Marion (2013), « *Une cause de riches ? L'accès des femmes au pouvoir économique* », Presses de Sciences Po. Sociétés contemporaines, vol. 89, no. 1, 2013, p. 101-130.

CIARAMELLA, Andrea, MIGLIORE, Alessandra, ROSSI-LAMASTRA, Cristina & TAGLIARO, Chiara, *Workplace management and gender: A literature review and a research agenda*. Working paper presented at the 4th RGCS symposium (23rd-24th January 2020, Lyon). Contribution published p. 133-136 in: GALLINA TOSCHI Tullia & BALZANO Angela & CRIVELLARO Francesca (eds.), *PLOTINA 2020 Conference. Book of Abstracts*, Bologna 2020. https://www.plotina.eu/wp-content/uploads/2020/04/PLOTINA-book-of-abstracts_FINAL-ISBN.pdf

DAHDAH, Assaf (2015). *Du Spatial turn au tournant géographique. Une brève introduction*. Ateliers doctoraux, Tournant spatial. https://jjctelemme.hypotheses.org/740

FABBRI, Julie (2015), *Les espaces de coworking pour entrepreneurs. Nouveaux espaces de travail et dynamiques interorganisationnelles collaboratives*, Thèse de doctorat en science de gestion, Centre de Recherche en Gestion, École Polytechnique, Palaiseau.

GARRETT, L. E., SPREITZER, G. M., & BACEVICE, P. A. (2017), *Co-constructing a sense of community at work: The emergence of community in coworking spaces*. Organization Studies, vol 38, n°6, p. 821-842.

MEROUEH, Saskia, *Julie Landour, Sociologie des Mompreneurs. Entreprendre pour concilier travail et famille ?*, Lectures, Les comptes rendus, 2019, mis en ligne le 24 juillet 2019. http://journals.openedition.org/lectures/36174

MITEV, Nathalie, DE VAUJANY, François-Xavie, LANIRAY, Pierre, BOHAS, Amélie & FABBRI, Julie. (2018). *Co-working spaces, collaborative practices and entrepreneurship. Chapter in Collaboration in the Digital Age*, edited by K. Riemer & S. Schellhammer, Springer Verlag, 2018.

PUYBARAUD, Marie (2017). *Workplace Powered by Human Experience. À global perspective*. http://humanexperience.jll/wp-content/uploads/2018/02/7686-JLL-HUMANEXPERIENCE_GLOBAL-REPORT_SPS_A4_V5.pdf

Novels, essays and collections

AMORUSO, Sophia. *#Girlboss*, Penguin, 2014.

CHANG, Emily, Brotopia: *Breaking Up the Boys' Club of Silicon Valley*, Portfolio, 2018.

LI, *Lu. Dear female founder: 66 Letters of Advice from Women Entrepreneurs Who Have Made $1 Billion in Revenue*, Blooming Founders Publishing, 2016.

VITAUD, Laëtitia. *Du Labeur à l'ouvrage*. Calman-Lévy, 2019.

VITAUD, Laëtitia. *Comment augmenter la place des femmes dans la tech ?* Livre blanc, Welcome to the Jungle, 2019

WOOLF, Virginia. *Une chambre à soi*. Hogarth Press, 1929.

Video

CoWomen, *How female spaces are transforming the (co) working world*, Coworking Europe Conference 2019, 13/11/2019. https://www.facebook.com/watch/live/?v=2683865095169883&ref=watch_permalink

Tools

The Community Canvas, A framework to help you build meaningful communities. https://community-canvas.org

Articles

Les « mumpreneuses », ces saintes mères de la start-up nation, Aurélia Blanc, Causette, Hors-Série #10 été 2019.
https://www.causette.fr/feminismes/au-lance-flammes/les-mumpreneuses-ces-saintes-meres-de-la-start-up-nation

Coworking non mixte : choix politique ou pragmatisme ?, Annabelle PERRIN, Socialter, Le guide des indépendants 2019 *Freelance, unissez-vous !* p 20-22. Octobre 2019.

Pourquoi le HUB Brussels n'est plus..., Anis BEDDA, 26 juin 2013, DESKMAG.
http://www.deskmag.com/fr/hub-brussels-coworking-modele-fermeture

London's first female-centric coworking space is in full bloom, Fastcompany, 08-07-18.
https://www.fastcompany.com/90214129/londons-first-female-centric-coworking-space-is-in-full-bloom

The business case for diversity in your workplace, Alex Ahom, November 26 2018, Medium.
https://medium.com/@shhared/the-business-case-for-diversity-in-your-workplace-162a947ae75e

The Wing Has $118 Million in Funding, Superfans Like Meryl Streep, and Plenty of Skeptics. It's Just Getting Started, INC Magazine, october 2019 issue (consulté le 1/03/2020).
https://www.inc.com/magazine/201910/christine-lagorio-chafkin/wing-audrey-gelman-women-coworking-space-network-community.html?cid=hmhero

Women-focused Coworking as a Current Business Trend, Helga MORENO, Andcards blog, January 27 2020.
https://www.andcards.com/blog/tips/women-focused-coworking/

A Coworking Space for Female Entrepreneurs, Stacey Sheppard, THEdesignSHEPPARD. blog, January 31 2020, with affiliate links.
https://www.thedesignsheppard.com/places/a-coworking-space-for-female-entrepreneurs#sthash.O0uxIJ65.ekQkbA6l.dpbs

The Wing Is a Women's Utopia. Unless You Work There. Amanda Hess, The New York Times, March 17 2020.
https://www.nytimes.com/2020/03/17/magazine/the-wing.html

WOMADE *(Bruxelles)*

©2020, Ivanne Poussier
Initially published in French under the title:
Soeurs d'armes, des femmes en quête d'espaces de coworking d'un genre nouveau

Edition : Ivanne Poussier
Impression : Ingramspark

ISBN : 978-2-9575303-0-4

Legal Deposit : October 2020

www.ingramcontent.com/pod-product-compliance
Lightning Source LLC
LaVergne TN
LVHW071807190726
843512LV00026B/674